END GAME

PROPHECY TODAY, WHAT YOU NEED TO KNOW

MATT COTE

This book is dedicated to my beautiful wife, Hannah, for her love and support. To my sons Elijah and Luke, I love you more than I thought I was capable of loving.

But ultimately, Jesus, this work is for you.

CONTENTS

INTRODUCTION

"The first time [Christ] came to slay sin in men. The second time He will come to slay men in sin." - Arthur W. Pink

Our world is changing rapidly. Everyday we have to filter through new information and discern whether or not what we are hearing is truth, intended for our benefit, or sensational distraction intended to instill a spirit of fear. It is extremely important that we have a spirit of discernment in this day and age. Not only do we need a spirit of discernment, we need knowledge of the Word of God, in particular, a general understanding of end times theology.

There is probably no greater need in the Body of Christ today than a general understanding of eschatology. Throughout the entire Kingdom, from Calvinist to Charismatic, the Holy Spirit is moving and telling our inner man that 'signs of the times' are upon us. Yet we [Christians] have probably never been more Biblically illiterate.

It is a tragedy of incomprehensible proportions.

We have come to care more about our cuffed jeans, pressed coffee and pristine social profile than the profound and sobering reality that God's judgement is coming. We in grace seem to forget that we too will stand before the King of Kings and will give an account for every idle word. In grace and covered by the atoning blood of Jesus we will be pardoned, yet speechless and awestruck toward Holiness that human thought can not even conceive.

In the Book of Revelation we are confronted with a Jesus that the world, and the Church, would hardly recognize. The meek and mild servant returns as a warrior ready for battle to finish once and for all the great war of the ages, to put an end to the insidious reign of that fallen angel, Lucifer, and to restore Kingdom order. Riding a horse and coming in splendor that would scare even the bravest of souls we meet the King of Kings in His awesome glory, the Creator of the universe in His final return, to take back what is rightfully His.

If that doesn't spark introspection, it should.

I was preaching at our church a few years back on the topic of spiritual maturity. Our boys, Elijah and Luke, were learning how to feed themselves and it was a period of time where Hebrews 5 came to life. What I am referring to is Hebrews 5:12-14 where it speaks about spiritual maturity and the correlation to feeding yourself. The author says this:

"For though by this time you ought to be teachers, you need someone to teach you again the basic principles of the oracles of God. You need milk, not solid food, for everyone who lives on milk is unskilled in the word of righteousness, since he is a child. **But solid food is for the mature, for those who have their powers of discernment trained by constant practice to distinguish good from evil.**" - Hebrews 5:12-14

In my study of the passage what stood out was the application to our day. A recent LifeWay Research study found that only 45 percent of those who regularly attend church read the Bible more than once a week. 1 in 5 said that they don't read the Bible at all. It creates a profound dilemma, that the children of God are malnourished or at best not growing as God intended. Because of this our churches and pastors are forced to hand out spiritual milk every week which leaves many hungry for more.

It also means that many are left ill-equipped, unable to discern the voice of God, to test the spirits and to lead others because they are handicapped by a system pandering to complacency and status quo.

One area of the Christian faith that has been especially impacted by this trend is the study of the end, or eschatology. I have been a student of eschatology for years but over the past several years, as our world has become more hostile and our nation more depraved, I have seen an increased hunger and thirst in Believers for information regarding what God says about the Last Days.

It is for this reason that I wrote this book.

This book was created to be a resource for you as we move forward in the coming years. There are specific markers and important anniversaries that are converging which point to significant, world altering change. Specifically, the purpose of this book is to help you grow in your discernment and understanding of end times scripture. We want to answer the following questions:

• How do we discern the information we are hearing?

• How can we approach the end times with a Biblical theology?

• If the Holy Spirit leads us into all truth, can the Holy Spirit illuminate scripture to give us modern day application?

We will look at and answer all of these questions.

We will also look at the telescopic nature of prophecy, what this means regarding initial and ultimate fulfillment and how it is unfolding today.

In particular we will look at nuclear proliferation and the 'end game' it presents. Not surprisingly, the end game of nuclear proliferation correlates with what the Bible says will occur in the Last Days. There is a major war in the Middle East that precedes the Tribulation. This war results in a peace treaty, or covenant, between Israel and its neighboring nations. It will be brokered by a political world leader along with the assistance of a religious world leader.

We will look at the prophecies of Daniel and Ezekiel, specifically Daniel 9 and Ezekiel 37-39. We will look at the application of Daniel 9 as it relates to the Triumphal Entry of Christ and the Siege of Jerusalem in 70 A.D. We will also look at the "pause" after the fulfillment of Daniel 9:26 and how the prophecies of Ezekiel bridge the gap between the destruction of the Second Temple to today.

Specifically we will look at what I call the "Ezekiel 37-39 Window". What is the Ezekiel 37-39 window? It is a period of time which spans the restoration and regathering of Israel through the Middle East war and ends with a covenant or peace treaty which was prophesied by Daniel in 9:27. It is of particular importance as it applies to the generation in which we live.

Prior to 1948 and the formation of the State of Israel differing theological viewpoints were presented regarding the Church and the status of Israel. Prior to the State of Israel the Jewish people were diaspora [or dispersed] and living in exile outside the Promised Land. Passages related to the 'Day of the Lord' or the latter days did not make sense because Israel did not exist. But what started through the Neo-Assyrian conquest of the Northern Kingdom of Israel in 740-722 B.C. and the subsequent exile of the Ten Lost Tribes would start a clock toward prophetic completion. The formal beginnings of this fulfillment would emerge after both World Wars and they continue today.

We will look at the big picture of history through the lens of scripture.

This book will bring everything together from the Assyrian Conquest of the Northern Kingdom of Israel and the first exile of the Jews to the present day regathering of Israel and current day events. We will look at the correlation between World War I and World War II, our current fight against ISIS and the emerging picture in the Middle East as a result of Arab Spring. We will also look at technology, how its linear curve and fixed trajectory give us a clear picture of our position within the Biblical timeline.

This will not be a book simply of academic study. Rather, this book will be a Holy Spirit driven work where I share what God has revealed through years of study, prayer and fasting while correlating it to proper exegesis, textual criticism and historical records.

My prayer is that after reading this book you will be able to test and discern what you hear on the news. That you will be better equipped to answer questions from both Christians and non-believers about the Last Days. That you will become a resource in your sphere of influence and an anchor when the storm comes, and yes, it is coming.

There is a difference between fear and preparation. One we are called to reject, the other we are called to pursue. Consider this a preparatory guide in the things which are to come, through which the purpose is to provide counsel so that in the "day of distress" you are prepared and at peace, a leader of resolve and fortitude.

CHAPTER 1

FOUNDATIONS

"We see the storm clouds gathering and events taking place that herald the second coming of Jesus Christ." - Billy Graham

The end, it has always been a controversial topic. While some are drawn with a fascination to the things which are to come others are repulsed, moving as far away as they can from the uncomfortable reality that our time is finite and our day could be interrupted at any moment by Christ's sovereign plan. The overwhelming majority of Christians live for the day without the slightest interruption of the Gospel in their daily life. They don't live for Christ or in light of eternity and His imminent return.

When confronted with difficult, prophetic passages they give a shrug and say, "No one knows the day or hour of Christ's return. We should live everyday in light of this reality".

However, their lives give no support to this claim.

The majority [of Christians] live in the world and are of it. Blended into a culture which Christ will judge they give little attention to the signs which are around them. But how could they, when the majority of Christians don't understand the very scriptures which explain them? Void of the Spirit's leading we find ourselves operating in the same spirit of confusion that is thrust on the world. When in reality the Revelation of God in scripture is a deep well of truth which is there for our understanding and delight. For if we follow the Lord He will lead. He will lead not only in the things which have happened, but also in the things which are to come.

Could it be that a proper walking out of our faith and the Gospel should be accompanied by an appropriate sense of urgency, knowing that the days are evil and that Christ's return is imminent? A belief that is lived out in spirit and truth? The early disciples lived this way, but as time has progressed each generation has taken hold of a sort of comfort, a mirage of distance and safety which leads to a false presumption: that nothing has happened for thousands of years therefore the same will be true for the next thousand years.

Not only is this calculation fool hearty it is in no way a Biblical response to the things which are to come. I would add, it is an assumption and comfort that we can not afford.

It was A.W. Tozer who said:

"Let us be alert to the season in which we are living. It is the season of the Blessed Hope, calling for us to cut our ties with the world and build ourselves on this One who will soon appear. He is our hope — a Blessed Hope enabling us to rise above our times and fix our gaze upon Him." 1

- A.W. Tozer, Preparing for Jesus' Return

But in order to fix our gaze we must first be awake. The question is, are we obedient in the harvest field or are we asleep, or perhaps, absent all together?

Setting the Stage

In order to begin we must set the stage. How can we begin to interpret that which generations have mishandled? How do we accurately divide the Word of Truth in this area? What is impossible for man is possible with God. We must not forget that this applies to everything, especially Biblical prophecy.

The answer is that through humility and the help of our Helper, the Holy Spirit, we can handle that which puts fear into the heart of man. Along with the help of our Lord we need proper textual criticism and an exegesis which applies proper context and historicity. In general we have to look at three main things:

• What does the Bible say? The specific, prophetic Revelation of God. The context and historicity.
• What are the opinions of man? The systematic theology or approaches to interpreting said scripture.
• What are the general revelations around us?

First, the Bible is the ultimate authority of all things. We will look directly at scripture and the context of each passage. Second, the Holy Spirit will lead us into all truth, even concerning what is to come. Over generations men have developed systematic approaches to the study of God (i.e. theology). We will look at the "study of the end" or eschatology and common viewpoints. Third, God's general revelation is all around us. Paul refers to this in Romans 1 when speaking to the evidence of God in creation. Aside from direct, prophetic Revelation in God's Word there is general insight that we can gather when in tune with the Holy Spirit.

This book is based on the premise that we are, in general, living in the Last Days. This of course speaking in generality to the days after the First Advent of Christ, His resurrection and ascension to Heaven.

To summarize, a correct Biblical worldview as it relates to eschatology involves a competent understanding of the scripture, general understanding of the systematic ways to approach it and a proper modern day application of the text.

A Biblical Theology

Before embarking on a subject as heavy and controversial as this I have to lay some theological groundwork. This isn't going to be a book based on speculation nor will it be an exhaustive study of each eschatological viewpoint. However, you will learn the basics. I will walk you through the basics of various eschatological viewpoints but also through how the Holy Spirit has illuminated scripture in my personal study.

To move forward you need to know that my goal is to let the Bible do the talking. To allow the Word of God to be the final word on everything, especially those things which occur in the end.

I have found from years of study that God has revealed certain pieces of truth to each denomination. We are the Body of Christ for a reason. I have found that not one denomination has it all figured out, rather, that each employs strengths which can [and often do] become equal weaknesses. That when theological study is done with the power of the Holy Spirit it actually brings a bond of peace and unity, clarity to the text and proper application. But this requires humility and the ability to see beyond pretense.

Because of this I have become a sort of Charismatic, Reformed Dispensational. That may confuse you, I understand, so let me explain.

I have found that allowing the Bible to lead over man-made systems brings ultimate clarity. The result is a theologically sound interpretation of scripture empowered by the Holy Spirit. That man-made systems can sometimes stifle the Spirit, that which allows the Word to breathe. In fact, you can have proper orthodoxy and orthopraxy while allowing the full expression of the Holy Spirit. In short, the Holy Spirit brings clarity to our faith from soteriology to eschatology. Similar to the red line of Christ through scripture, when the Holy Spirit is accurately expressed we see a complete and theologically sound picture of the Christian faith.

Neither the lack of theology nor the worship of it are Biblical, rather, both extremes are idolatry and an equal curse.

In other words, the Holy Spirit has authority over Calvin and Darby. So we must approach the Word of God with the Holy Spirit as the ultimate authority, not with set pretense. We forget this and often allow commentaries and interpretation of man to trump the authority of the Holy Spirit. In this we end up creating a man-made idol. It is possible for men to be wrong, but it is impossible for God to be wrong. So the dangers of following a man-made system too closely make us subject to a stumbling block which prevents us from drawing out of the deep well of truth [the Bible] that which only the Holy Spirit can do.

"When the Spirit of truth comes, **He will guide you into all the truth,** for He will not speak on His own authority, but whatever He hears He will speak, and **He will declare to you the things that are to come.** He will glorify me, for He will take what is mine and declare it to you." - John 16:13-14

Did you catch that?

The Holy Spirit declares to us the "things that are to come". We miss this for many reasons. Either because we are too busy, too engrained in pretense or we lack the faith to follow His lead. But just as God tells us not to throw pearls before swine, God doesn't give His best information to fools.

To the intellectual this means that this passage in John 16 is not Charismatic, it is the Word of God and it applies to you too.

Our [Christian] generation has become one of emotion and speculation, it is the result of ignorance. I understand the tragedy of heretical teaching from the pulpit today but that is not what I am offering you here. We are not negating the role of sound doctrine and right theology, but particularly as it relates to eschatology, we are allowing the Holy Spirit to lead us into right application. There is probably no place more important to keep this in mind than the study of eschatology.

My goal is to keep this book and its language within reach for laymen, but I also want theologians to be informed of its foundation. So to better understand the theological backdrop of this work I put it into four simple points.

1. **The Holy Spirit does the work of salvation.** Repentance is not possible without the Holy Spirit, meaning any action tied to receiving Christ is ultimately a supernatural draw that we can take no credit for. In other words, it is hard to take credit for the words of my mouth when I can't take credit for the breath in my lungs! However, even though Christ chose the disciples they had to respond to His call. They had to make a decision to leave everything and follow Him. There is a tension of sovereignty and free will that will never be fully understood, this antinomy is necessary and good for it keeps us humble and reminds us of our designed limitations. I would lean towards a reformed soteriology, giving emphasis to the work of the Holy Spirit. It is not about me or my effort, even in repentance, it is the work of Christ in me.

2. **The Holy Spirit seals you to the day of redemption.** Just as you are physically born once, you are spiritually born once. This blessed assurance of salvation is sealed through the Holy Spirit. Meaning, the elect will endure and persevere.

We are in a process of sanctification and not in our glorified state, so the Spirit is constantly at war with the flesh. The more I surrender to the Spirit the more I have victory over the flesh. The more I die to self and surrender my life to Christ, the more the Spirit can move and shine through me. My shortcomings and failures after conversion don't remove my status as a child of God. Since we don't know who is unregenerate or simply backslidden, we are not to judge, but rather to exhort and encourage all who claim to be in Christ to live as we are called.

3. **The Holy Spirit leads us into all truth.** Most Christians understand the theological importance of the Holy Spirit but many miss altogether the practical importance of the Holy Spirit. Meaning, they read the Bible as text rather than what it is: the living, breathing, Word of God. The Word is alive! Alive means that He is actively speaking and the application is for our day. Once you have a solid theological foundation you need to learn how to discern the voice of God. Many don't know how to listen to or discern the voice of God. This is the breeding ground of dead religion. The Word is alive, which means God still speaks! As you meditate on God's Word He will lead you, but you have to draw near to Him. As you hear from God the Word of God will help you discern and test the spirits. The Sword of the Spirit is how you separate what is true from what is false. So open it, read it, study it and meditate on it, God will lead you in how to apply it.

4. **The Holy Spirit is not an object of God's wrath.** Although trial and tribulation, often severe, will come upon the Christian we are not an object of God's wrath. God does

not wage war against Himself. Since we possess and are sealed by the Holy Spirit we [Christians] are not objects of God's wrath. But we are enemies of Satan, which makes us a target in this war. So it is possible to endure great tribulation and not be an object of God's wrath. There is a difference between suffering and wrath, although we are not an object of God's wrath we will share in Christ's suffering.

The goal is that we are living each day as we should, also that we are not ignorant with what the Bible says regarding the end. **Living each day for Christ doesn't mean we are allowed ignorance of any part of scripture.** Rather, that we are knowledgeable and ready to lead others when they have questions. If we are surrendered to the Holy Spirit He will lead us, however we need to trust His leadership and not our own intellect or emotions.

The Bible is a deep well of truth and the Holy Spirit is our Helper to draw it out.

In short, if you are seminary educated, Reformed, Charismatic, Dispensational.... this book is for you. It may not agree with every facet of your pretense, but that is okay. The purpose is to share what the Holy Spirit has revealed to me through prayer, fasting and personal study. It is for your own personal study and cross reference. It is also for the layperson to gain a general understanding of what the Bible says about the Last Days.

For those worried that this book won't have a theological foundation, don't worry it will. For those worried that it will be an intellectual pursuit void of the Holy Spirit, don't worry it won't. God is doing a new thing in our generation and He is drawing men and women closer to Himself. With Christ at the center He brings us all together, it is inevitable. This book may stretch you, at least that is my hope, and that exercise is good for the Body.

Systems of Theology

What you believe doesn't matter.

Yes, you read that right. We are going to destroy some sacred idols here. Let me follow up that statement with conjoining truth so that it is complete and satisfying.

It doesn't matter what you believe, it matters that what you believe in is true.

You can have the faith of a giant but if wrongly placed it means nothing. The validity of the faith is based on the object, not the strength of the faith. We know and understand this across false religions. We know that there are many false religions throughout the world, with followers stronger in faith than most Christians, however they have placed their faith into something that doesn't save. At the end of the day it doesn't matter how much faith they have, it matters that they place their faith in the right person, Jesus.

An obvious example of this is the faith of Islam. Probably no other world religion offers such faith, such pilgrimage, such willingness to lay down ones life, even if in such a sick and twisted way. However, it doesn't matter how much faith a person has in Allah, the faith is misplaced. Jesus is more than a prophet, He is God. Since their faith is in the wrong object it has no merit or saving power. The same applies to Biblical study.

It doesn't matter what we believe about the Bible, it matters that what we believe about the Bible is true.

It is funny that we as Christians know this principle to be true when analyzing false religions, yet we fall prey to it in our own study of God. Many find themselves entrenched in a school of thought, a systematic theology or Spirit filled pretense, either because it was how they were raised or what they were taught in seminary. They purpose that what they believe is true simply for the reason that they believe it. Yet that couldn't be further from the truth!

Actually, the many schools of thought in theology present an obvious dilemma: not all of them are true.

Each theological approach gives us a piece of truth, they are true in part, but not the whole. That is why we are the Body of Christ, because our weakness is the other brother's strength. We need each other.

This is a sobering reality and something that isn't given enough thought. It doesn't matter how many people are in your camp or that we are surrounded by people that believe the same things as we do. Rather, we need to look at all the theological systems, those which are rooted in sound doctrine, and ask ourselves the hard questions, "Could the system I ascribe to be wrong? If so, in what area and am I humble enough to change my stance?".

This applies to all of us, from the Calvinist to the Charismatic. Could the cessationist be wrong about the Holy Spirit? Could the supernatural saint use a better theology? The answer is a resounding, yes.

But in order to discern what may be right or wrong you need the Holy Spirit and an understanding of what each viewpoint says. In our Biblically illiterate culture this void creates a vacuum. We have become more polarized today rather than a more complete picture of Christ. This war being waged in the Body is a sign of sickness. But this sickness can be cured through repentance, love and understanding.

Since all camps have strengths and weaknesses it is wise to learn what they all offer and ask the Holy Spirit to refine the dross. As it relates to eschatology we need to begin by looking at all viewpoints and then allow the Holy Spirit to put the pieces of the puzzle together.

Schools of Thought

Below is a brief overview of the schools of thought regarding eschatology, or the study of the end.

Eschatology is a major branch of Christian theology which studies the scripture regarding the end of the age. The word "eschatology" is derived from two Greek words which mean "last" (ἔσχατος) and "study" (-λογία). 2

The study of eschatology covers the issues of death, afterlife, Heaven, Hell, the Second Advent (Coming) of Jesus, Resurrection, Rapture, Tribulation, Millennialism, the Last Judgement and the New Heaven and Earth which are to come. Regarding the approaches to studying the end we will look at the main four. They include Preterism, Historicism, Futurism and Idealism.

Preterism - Preterism is derived from the Latin word praeteritus, meaning "gone by". Preterists, whether Full or Partial, believe that prophecy has mostly been fulfilled in centuries past. In particular, they view the Book of Revelation as either symbolic prophetic presentation or having been fulfilled in the first century. In short, this approach bases that many of the Bible's prophecies were fulfilled during the life and time of Jesus and the Early Church.

Historicism - Similar to Preterism, Historicism is an approach which sees prophecy as historical but also as present and future, during the previous two millennia. For example, Historicists believe the Great Tribulation has already occurred during the Papal supremacy from 538-1798. The Book of Revelation is largely believed to be a vision which combined secular and ecclesiastical history of Christendom during the political changes of the Roman world.

Futurism - Probably the most widely held belief or eschatological structure in modern day Christianity. This viewpoint was popularized by Dispensational theologians. This was due in part to the rise of Dispensationalism in America and its influence around the world. In Futurism, eschatological prophecies are referring to events which have not yet been fulfilled but will take place at the end of the age.

Idealism - Idealism is the spiritual or non-literal approach to prophetic scriptures. The Book of Revelation and other prophetic passages are viewed and interpreted symbolically. For example, the Beast and Babylon are represented as social injustices and view the recreation of the earth as "general improvement to society".

So, where would this writing be placed in these approaches?

This work would be placed in the Futurist approach to end times scripture. That end times prophecy is just that, prophecy about the very end. That the "Day of the Lord" has not occurred yet, Christ has not returned, so previous fulfillment of the passages was preliminary foreshadowing and not ultimate fulfillment. There is a clear difference between the Church and Israel in scripture and prophetic passages surrounding the end are directed to the people of Israel. In this capacity the book will be in line with Dispensational views as it relates to Israel and the Church.

However as it relates to the coming of the Lord, or the rapture of the saints, it would be more in line with Reformed teaching. This based solely on Biblical account. This is perhaps the centerpiece of the work and what I believe to be the most important message for this generation.

But the main focus of this book is the period of time in which we live.

My focus is to look at prophecies that have implications for our day. Specifically Daniel 9 and the telescopic nature of that passage in conjunction with the prophetic implications of Ezekiel 37-39, which speaks to the regathering and restoration of Israel at the end of the Time of the Gentiles (Luke 21). They are multi-faceted and give us a wealth of understanding. We will look at the words of Jesus in the Olivet Discourse and through proper textual criticism apply the words of Paul to the Thessalonians and the Revelation John received on the Island of Patmos.

This will give us clear insight into how prophetic passages surrounding Israel are applicable in our day. Also, it will give us clear insight into future events such as the restoration of Israel, the Magog wars, the Tribulation and the ultimate return of Christ.

But before we dig into these passages, before we look at their historic significance and future implications, we need to start with an unlikely source for insight.

Technology.

Yes, you read that right. Although technology is not something commonly talked about in regards to prophetic scripture it should be and I will explain why in the next chapter.

CHAPTER 2

THE TECHNOLOGY GAUGE

"In the end knowledge will increase, technology is a means to an end." - Anonymous

Many people shy away from eschatology or anything related to end times prophecy primarily because few people are eager to meet Jesus right now. I mean, who wants to eagerly await the end of this life? I will tell you who... those who are poor, suffering and waiting for release from the bondage of human existence. Hard for many of us in America to understand but millions around the world live in conditions that we can not fathom, many wait for Christ to return with imminence because they are suffering to an extent to which we can not fully comprehend. They make up the "least of these" mentioned by Jesus in Matthew 25. They are important because how we treat them is of particular significance to God at the Judgement Seat of Christ.

I will never forget my trip to Africa in 2007 when I encountered an AIDS hospice in Lusaka, Zambia. It was run by the Catholic Church and we were invited to do a walk through as a part of our mission trip, a group of senior and local pastors from the United States.

What I encountered changed my life.

Young girls, no older than their early teens, were in the latter stages of the AIDS virus taking over their body. Many had been raped by men in their villages through counsel of a local witch doctor. It was believed by pagans in the area that having sex with a virgin would cleanse your HIV/AIDS infection. However, we know this is just Satanic myth.

The long but narrow room had no air conditioning, many were throwing up into buckets next to their bed. Christian nurses assisted some out of bed for their daily shower. I was pale, my spirit crushed, my stomach in knots. I had to step outside.

I will never forget that moment. The smell in the air of fires being burnt in the ghettos across the street. The beautiful sunset in the sky as I looked up to the heavens and said...

"Jesus, come quickly".

Maybe you've had a similar moment, either through personal suffering or suffering that you have encountered in other peoples lives, where you could see the state of fallen man and the results of sin so clearly that if Jesus returned in that moment you would be okay with not accomplishing all that you had set out to do in life.

A moment of awakening, where the need for Jesus trumped every internal desire.

But other than our lack of need for Jesus in everyday life, due to physical comfort and complacency which liberty in

America affords, the abundance of false teaching and false prophecy has led many to turn away entirely from the study of the end [eschatology]. Many false teachings have been used over the years to incite fear or the opposite, to create apathy.

We need neither fear nor flight but rather resolve and understanding, through which the Holy Spirit can do mighty things.

I am not trying to incite fear into the hearts of my readers but rather to inform you so that you are armed. Information is the most powerful weapon on earth. There is a reason why men and governments fight so hard to obtain it.

The information we seek is from the Holy Spirit. We want His guidance and illumination into our study of the scriptures. For without it we may as well be lost in the woods. We have laid the groundwork of theology and now to move forward we need to understand better the time in which we live, specifically, our position in history.

Our Place in History

Did you know that the biggest battles are yet to be fought?

I don't mean military engagements between nations, although the same would be true for those, I am referring to war in the spiritual realms. That the spiritual battles we will fight in the years ahead will be ones of legend. What we read in the Bible is possible today, the story isn't finished yet... the best is yet to come.

That breathes life into the heart of a warrior. That we are in an age of greatness and that the opportunity for men and women to achieve it through humble obedience to Christ is obtainable. God is raising up men and women for just a time as this.

We are alive at a very strategic moment in history and there is no better way to gauge our trajectory and current position than with technology.

Let me explain.

The Technology Gauge

Technology isn't going away, in fact, the advancement of technology will just continue to accelerate. You may be wondering, "What is a chapter on technology doing in a book about eschatology?". The answer is this: the two go hand in hand.

There are two primary reasons for addressing technology as it relates to eschatology and they are as follows:

1. **Because the future global platform, which is prophesied in scripture, will be built on technology.** The global economy, border control, purchasing, medical records and the proliferation of information, in particular the Gospel, are built on technology.

2. **Technology is linear and accelerating.** It gives clear trajectory and timing. I will explain this in more detail later.

Did you know that technology is not subject to the Law of Diminishing Returns? Most people don't realize that technology is not subject to the Law of Diminishing Returns, or at least the true effects of this law on technology are contested. In economics this is also known as the Law of Variable Proportions, the Principle of Diminishing Marginal Productivity or Diminishing Marginal Return.

What the Law of Diminishing Returns, a fundamental principle in economics, states is this: "in all productive processes, adding more of one factor of production, while holding all others constant ("ceteris paribus"), will at some point yield lower incremental per-unit returns". 3

However, it doesn't fully apply to technology in the aggregate. Why is this and what are the implications?

It is because technology in and of itself is always increasing, it never retreats but always advances. It is in a state of perpetual growth. Of course, this is when applied to technology itself and not a product of technology. Technology products have life cycles whereas technology is always evolving and growing.

An example of this would be cassette tapes, VHS and DVDs vs the internet and digital distribution. Whereas the cassette tape, VHS and DVD have all reached the end of their life cycle, they gave birth to the next phase of technological growth, which is digital distribution. Here is a graph known as a logarithmic plot to demonstrate.

4. Graph Commons: Courtesy of Ray Kurzweil via Wiki Commons

In futures studies and the history of technology this is known as **accelerating change**. In short, accelerating change means that the growth trend of technology is exponential and is accelerating rather than diminishing. It was because of this that Ray Kurzweil proposed the Law of Accelerating Returns. It means that whenever technology comes across a barrier it forces a paradigm shift, which just births the next piece of technology and allows it to cross through and break that barrier.

Up to this point the theorem has been proven accurate and true. This is why social scientists are so concerned about artificial intelligence and the trajectory that technology presents for mankind. In fact, in his 1999 book The Age of Spiritual Machines, Kurzweil proposes that this exponential growth pattern and accelerating change present the possibility of technological singularity by the year 2045.

What does technological singularity mean?

It means the point where machine intelligence would have the capability to overtake human intelligence. Yep, that is a Hollywood movie plot twist there. This is why Stephen Hawking, Elon Musk and Bill Gates among others have all come out recently and warned about the dangers of AI. It is also why The X Prize Foundation and IBM just announced [February 2016] a new global X Prize competition with a focus on artificial intelligence. 5

Mass Use of Inventions
Years Until Use by 1/4 U.S. Population

Logarithmic Plot

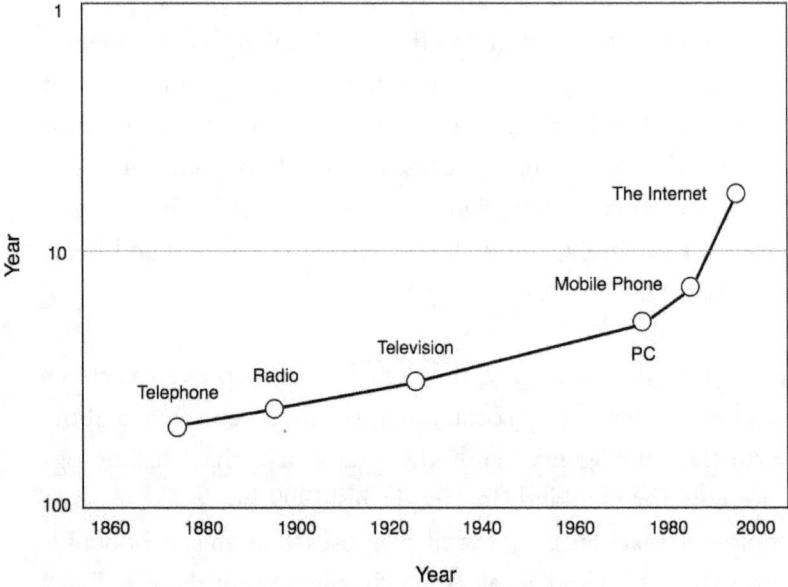

Now, we as Christians are not afraid because we know that God has a plan and we are trusting in Him.

The reason for bringing all of this up is this: **the growth of technology is linear which means we can track it. We can not only track it, we know its trajectory.**

Many will look at earthquakes, wars, rumors of wars and natural disasters as an inferred barometer of the times in which we live. They try to correlate these events to end times passages and suggest that the "Day of the Lord" is near. However, it is flawed logic and an uninformed viewpoint. More importantly, it is a practice that evidences both the leadership of fear and the absence of the Holy Spirit. The problem is that these events ebb and flow throughout history and give no true indication that we are in the Last Days. There is no clear and defined pattern therefore they give no clear reference point.

However, technology is different.

Technology not only gives us trend it gives us trajectory. An example of this would be currency.

Let's say for example you look at the evolution of money and the impacts of technology since the life of Abraham (1813 B.C.). We went from barter exchange (livestock, etc) and precious metals such as gold and silver to paper fiat currency, bank accounts, credit cards and now digital disruption, meaning Bitcoin and digital currency. The global economy, wearable technology and numerical systems associated with persons provide the environment of prophetic fulfillment. **This trajectory has a destination and that destination is Biblical, prophetic fulfillment.**

It is Accelerating Change which pushes us over the threshold. We know that over the next 10 years we will see advancement that will surpass, in both size and scope, the technological advancements of the last 10 years. Factoring in where we stand on the linear graph of technology and where it is headed based on the Law of Accelerating Returns, we know that the rate of change in technology will increase exponentially and will usher us into new systems of monetary exchange, information transfer, border control, etc.

Technology is important because it provides a means to an end. It is how information or "knowledge will increase" (Daniel 12:4) during the end, how the global system is born and how the world becomes interconnected during the Last Days.

In short, the linear curve of technology is taking us somewhere, it has a clear and defined trend and that destination is Biblical. Technology by nature does not ebb or flow and gives us a clear and defined trajectory, one we must be knowledgeable about and should pay attention to. We don't place our hope or faith there, we also don't use it to time events. But we need to understand the fundamental nature of technology and know that as signs emerge, which present an environment capable of a one world system, they are emerging for a reason.

Most importantly, God is using technology to get the Gospel to the nations. A major paradigm shift that impacted the Church was the advent of the Gutenberg Press circa 1440. This new technology allowed the Bible to be printed and proliferated around the world. Not so surprisingly it preceded of The Reformation, a milestone event for the Church in the West and the movement of the Gospel. Similar to this breakthrough is that of the Internet, which is enabling the Gospel to reach the world and is taking us into the next era of Gospel movement.

Because of this, even on a practical level, technology is very important to the Church.

Modern Warfare

This technological jargon may not be of interest to you but it has important ramifications. Technology may seem benign when applied to video games, media and mobile communication however it becomes more significant and severe when applied to military advancement and modern warfare. What I am speaking to is the advent of nuclear technology after World War II. It was a paradigm shift of such magnitude that it places us into an era of prophetic fulfillment.

To begin to unpack the Bible and to study the end, or what is to come, we have to understand what has already occurred. In other words, we have to look at history in order to gain a proper perspective of the future. Going forward we will look at historical events, both by secular and Biblical account, and how they prove past prophecies as true. We will also look at what this means for future fulfillment.

Over the next few chapters we will look at both World Wars, how they fulfilled Biblical prophecy and what it means for the future. We will also look at the prophecies of old and their fulfillment. Specifically, the prophecies of Jeremiah, Daniel and Ezekiel, the prophetic words of Jesus and the vision given to John on the Island of Patmos.

It should be of no surprise that everything in scripture, when viewed in proper context, submits to the words of Jesus. That the prophecies of old were fulfilled with supernatural accuracy and that fulfillment of future prophecy will occur in like manner.

So to begin our study of the future we must first unpack the past.

CHAPTER 3

THE BIG PICTURE

"The only thing new in the world is the history you do not know."
- Harry S. Truman

Growing up my family would occasionally do jigsaw puzzles. Now, I am a child of the 80's so this was before technology dominated everyday life. My dad would lay out a puzzle on the kitchen table and we would work at it piece by piece. The larger the puzzle and the more pieces it had, the longer it would take for the picture to come together. The same applies to prophecy. In order to see the big picture, to see what the pieces are coming together to form, you have to step back.

To see the big picture you need the right perspective.

Since the Financial Crisis of 2008 people have become more aware of our changing world. It is becoming more evident that we live in a global system where economic and social factors bleed across borders. This connection has been made possible due to technology, namely the Internet, which makes the world a smaller and more centralized place. It was after this watershed event, where financial contagion brought the world to the brink of financial disaster, when people started to take notice of trends. Specifically, the 7 year sabbatical cycle and its implied impact on our world.

Because of this in 2015 many expected significant events to occur during the Shemitah [or 7 year sabbatical cycle] and I was one of them. But nothing happened. In fact we sailed right through September and October of 2015 unscathed. So was the sabbatical cycle correlation unfounded? Is it merely superstition and myth or did we miss something, something much bigger?

I will explain in later chapters the importance of the Shemitah and Jubilee Year but before we get there we need to understand what we are witnessing today. What we are witnessing today is called convergence. It is when multiple factors come together and point to larger, ultimate fulfillment.

You could call it a perfect storm.

Similar aspects of convergence preceded both World Wars. Be that financial, social or geo-political. Since cycles repeat themselves we know that the past can be indicative of the future. History gives us insight into the future. As mentioned above with the example of the jigsaw puzzle, when analyzing prophetic scripture you have to take the pieces of information God is giving you and step back in order to gain the proper perspective. If you aren't seeing what you need to, or it is confusing, you are probably standing too close.

In this case we need to step back 100 years to the time period of World War I.

The World Wars

When you look back at history you will notice that wars, like storms, are catalysts for change. Not only do they lead to the rise and fall of civilizations but they also bring about the fulfillment of God's plan for His people. Whether it was the Fall of Babylon to the Persian Empire in October of 539 B.C. and the subsequent return of the Jews from exile to Judah, or the Siege of Jerusalem in 70 A.D. and the implications it has for the Church, the new temple of God. Wars, or geopolitical change, have historically been tied to Biblical, prophetic fulfillment.

Because of this we need to take seriously the prophetic implications of the recent World Wars. When you look at them and what they accomplished through a Biblical worldview you see an amazing picture. These two monumental wars of the last century were not simply fought to extinguish the flames of a tyrannical regime, but were used to repossess the Holy Land and restore the people of Israel.

In short, they were 'perfect storms' which brought about world altering change and prophetic fulfillment. Let's take a closer look.

World War 1 – Retrieve Palestine from Ottoman Rule.

Before World War I the Ottoman Empire controlled much of the Mediterranean region including modern day Greece, Palestine (or the Holy Land) and northern Africa. But it would be through World War I where this controlling power in the Middle East would be conquered. The Empire's defeat as a result of World War I would lead to the formation of a new state, modern day Turkey, and as a result of the Allied victory land was redistributed to create the modern day formation of the Middle Eastern states.

Of unique importance to today is the connection between the Ottoman Caliphate and the current day emergence of ISIS or ISIL. As World War I broke out the Young Turks government (Ottoman Empire) made an alliance with Germany, entering the war on the side of the Central Powers. It was in November of 1914 when the Ottoman Empire would declare military jihad against France, Russia and Great Britain. As stated above, the Empire [Ottoman] would fall, leading also to the fall of the Ottoman Caliphate. The Ottoman Caliphate, under the dynasty of the Ottoman Empire, would be the last Sunni Islamic caliphate. After World War I the Turkish Grand National Assembly under the direction of first Turkish President Mustafa Kemal Atatürk would declare an end to the Khalifate, declaring:

"The Khalifa has no power or position except as a nominal figurehead." 6

It is disputed to this day among Islamic extremists and has subsequently led to the rise of ISIS or ISIL, which is trying to restore the Ottoman Caliphate. Not only is this in direct defiance to the sovereignty of Turkey it contests to restore what World War I abolished, which is Sunni supremacy in the Levant under the direction of the Caliphate.

World War I started everything we are seeing today. It was this war which led to the reorganizing and partitioning of the Middle East. Lines were drawn, territories were moved but specifically the British conquered Palestine from the Ottoman Empire, thus giving control of the region to the British.

The Allied victory of World War I led to the formation of new countries in Europe and the Middle East. Namely, it transferred regions of the former Ottoman Empire to other powers. The French would gain control over Syria and Lebanon. The British would control most of Ottoman Mesopotamia (Iraq) and Ottoman Syria which includes Palestine. The territory, called Mandatory Palestine, would remain under British rule from 1920-1948.

This would set up World War II and everything it would accomplish.

World War 2 – Unite the Nations [United Nations], Place Israel in the Holy Land

World War I had radically altered the world map. Pacifism was a widely held sentiment following the war however revolution in Germany would eventually lead to the rise of the Nazi regime. Although related conflicts started earlier, World War II would begin in September of 1939 and end in September of 1945.

As a result of World War II the United Nations was formed. The British would then hand over Mandate Palestine to the UN for land distribution and settlement. On November 29,1947 the UN General Assembly voted in favor of Resolution 181 which adopted the plan for the partition of Palestine. Six months later Israel was established on May 14, 1948.

Through the lens of hindsight and a Biblical worldview we can see the progression and connection of both World Wars. By standing back we gain proper perspective to see the bigger picture of what God was doing.

The connection is Israel.

First, the Holy Land had to be repossessed (World War I) then it had to be redistributed (World War II). Both of these large scale, world wars, were ultimately about the Jews and the Nation of Israel being restored. They were large scale storms which altered the world map and fulfilled Biblical prophecy. It was the beginning of a large scale undoing of Jewish exile and brought about the restoration of not only the State of Israel but the regathering of the Jewish people.

But just as the end of World War I was a set up for World War II and everything it would accomplish, the way in which World War II ended gives us insight into the next and final world wars.

The Game Changer

The nuclear weapon was a game changer.

Introduced through military engagement at the end of World War II in August of 1945, the nuclear bomb is an explosive device which derives its destructive force from nuclear reaction, be that fission (the fission bomb) or a combination of fission and fusion (the thermonuclear weapon). Weapons of this nature are considered "WMD" or "Weapons of Mass Destruction". Also included in this category would be any chemical, biological or other weapon which can bring about significant destruction or harm, causing extreme damage to humans, buildings and civilization as a whole.

Hence the title and cover of this book, nuclear technology presents a specific 'end game' which ties directly to end times prophecy.

When you have a weapon which can bring about 'the end of civilization as we know it', it creates the need for centralized leadership [United Nations] in which world leaders, under the direction of the head, can legislate and prevent its use. The weapon itself is just a forerunning element of diplomacy and centralized world leadership. In other words, the advent of nuclear technology at the end of World War II made a united world government a necessity, forcing the hand of ultimate diplomacy and the creation of the United Nations.

The advent of nuclear technology and the United Nations at the end of World War II was no coincidence. It brought about two things needed for world peace: a weapon to force the hand and the leadership or mediating faction to broker the covenant. By placing Jews in Palestine and giving them a weapon which can 'end all war' it places ultimate power into the hands of the mediator, or the entity which created the sovereignty of the Nation of Israel. Giving a similar weapon to Iran, or the spiritual domain of the Prince of Persia, just completes the ingredients necessary for catalytic change. It forces the hand of peace and the covenant mentioned in Daniel 9.

Nuclear Game Theory

A weapon of such magnitude in the hands of both the aggressor and defender presents a profound dilemma, neither have the incentive to pull the trigger.

In 1867 Alfred Nobel [Nobel Peace Prize] stated that "the day when two army corps can annihilate each other in one second, all civilized nations, it is to be hoped, will recoil from war and discharge their troops". He was ahead of his time. What Nobel was referring to was "a super weapon that would put an end to all war" 7 as Nikola Tesla put it in 1937. The introduction of the nuclear weapon at the end of World War II was such a weapon.

Nuclear weaponry creates a stalemate known in game theory as Mutual Assured Destruction or MAD. MAD is a doctrine of military strategy, based on the theory of deterrence, which holds that when both the attacker and defender have the power to annihilate each other it prevents the enemy's use of those same weapons. It is a Nash equilibrium where neither side have an incentive to disarm or initiate conflict. We have been in such an equilibrium since the end of World War II. 8

However status quo is changing and we see similar signs emerging, rumblings reminiscent of the days which preceded the wars of the past, and it points to a future world-wide engagement.

The emergence of ISIS [or ISIL] is bringing back the quest for a Sunni Caliphate. Marching across the Levant ISIS is on an mission to restore the Caliphate of the Ottoman Empire all the while maintaining control over a large section of Eastern Syria.

Economic sanctions have now been removed from Iran, raising concerns in the international community about increased funding for its nuclear program. The removal of sanctions also raising concerns that it will lead to increased financial support of the extremist group Hezbollah, a group to which Iran has been a long time supporter.

The "red line" between Iran and Israel has been crossed leaving Israel to defend itself, seemingly alone, as relations with the United States are on the decline.

Russia, which carved its way through the Black Sea region, now occupies Georgia (2008), annexed Crimea (2014) and neutralized Eastern Ukraine in what is being called the "silent secession of eastern Ukraine". Russian military has recently been operating in Syria and staged to help support their ally who has been fighting a civil war since March of 2011. Russian troops were withdrawn in early 2016, yet days later Vladimir Putin stated that planes would be mobilized within hours to support Assad leaving the door open for further aggression in the region.

These moves in the Middle East are increasing tension to the Nash equilibrium and they happen to be occurring a few years before major markers of Biblical completion. Lines that were drawn as a result of World War I are being challenged, bringing the world together into what is being called "a proto-world war with nearly a dozen countries embroiled in two overlapping conflicts" 9.

The question is not a matter of if but when it becomes official.

Our Place in History

Looking back at history through the lens of hindsight and a Biblical worldview we know that both World Wars were more than just the result of geo-political unrest, but a catalyst for prophetic fulfillment. The Ottoman Empire was conquered, the Holy Land repossessed and the Jews regathered, placed back in their homeland and united as one nation (Ezekiel 37:22).

It bring us into the Ezekiel 37-39 Window, which I will document in later chapters.

We are now approaching significant markers and anniversaries that point to the next stages of prophetic fulfillment.

In 2018 we will witness the 100 year anniversary of the end of World War I along with the 70 year anniversary of the State of Israel. More than just markers, these are milestones which tell the reader to wake up and pay attention to the events in the Middle East which seek to unravel all that God has accomplished for Israel. We know that this won't happen. Rather, that moves being made at the epicenter are merely a setup for what is next in God's plan for the world. It is not just our place in history or our position on the linear curve of the technology which should prompt a response, but also where we stand on the sabbatical timeline and by that I mean the Shemitah (sabbatical) and Jubilee calendar.

In later chapters I will share my research into the Shemitah and Jubilee cycles. How the timing of events in the Middle East are of no coincidence. But first we need to look at how Israel came to be exiled from their land in the first place. We need to step back even further to the exile of the Northern Kingdom of Israel in 740 B.C., for it was this exile which set everything into motion.

We will look at this in the next chapter.

CHAPTER 4

THE BIGGER PICTURE

"The farther backward you can look, the farther forward you are likely to see." - Winston S. Churchill

If history isn't your cup of tea I hope this book sparks a bit of interest, because it is of utmost importance. The more we know about our past the more insight we will gain about our future. This is true in the sense that men tend to forget things, our amnesia occurs generationally, but it is also important because prophecy builds upon itself.

Biblical prophecy is known to be "telescopic" or having at least a dual fulfillment. This means there is typically an immediate and ultimate fulfillment of Biblical prophecy. Many schools of eschatology focus on the first [historical application] when in reality there is a larger, ultimate fulfillment that is yet to be accomplished.

It is simple, although we make it more complicated than it ought to be. Passages of scripture speaking to the "Day of the Lord" are speaking of future events because the "Day of the Lord" has not occurred yet.

Remember the analogy of the jigsaw puzzle we used in the previous chapter? Well, let's step back even further to gain the benefit of an even better perspective. Although it is great to see the connection between both World Wars and the restoration of modern day Israel, we need to step back even further in Israel's history.

Before we look at the historical exiles and returns of the Jewish people and the prophecies surrounding them we have to go back to creation and understand the cycles God put in place at the beginning of the foundations of the earth. It is because God's Law is built on top of these cycles and the correlation helps us understand the implications of disobeying God's Laws. It will also help us understand key prophecies and why certain events, such as the Shemitah and Jubilee Year, are correlated to the discipline and land of the Jewish people.

Genesis - Starting the Clock

It doesn't go any further back than Creation and we need to start with day four of the Creation account. Although light had been separated from darkness time keeping, or time telling, had not yet been created. In Genesis Chapter 1 we see God do just that.

"Then God said, "Let there be lights in the expanse of the heavens to separate the day from the night, **and let them be for signs and for seasons and for days and years**; and let them be for lights in the expanse of the heavens to give light on the earth"; and it was so. God made the two great lights, the greater light to govern the day, and the lesser light to govern the night; He made the stars also. God placed them in the expanse of the heavens to give light on the earth, and to govern the day and the night, and to separate the light from the darkness; and God saw that it was good. There was evening and there was morning, a fourth day." - Genesis 1:14-19

Here on the fourth day of creation God creates the sun and moon and the ability to track time. In His miraculous omniscience we see objects that tell the time of day and the time of the month. The sun, which rises in the East and sets in the West, tells daily time on a sun dial. The moon, which acts as a satellite to give light during the night, tells monthly time through lunar cycles. Both are used for signs and seasons.

God built everything on cycles.

We who use the Gregorian calendar can miss this however Jews, those who use the Hebrew or lunar calendar, understand its importance. Hebrew historians and time keepers have been using it since creation to track history and time. So what are the cycles and how do they matter Biblically?

Sets of 7

In short, the cycle is based on sets of 7 and builds on itself. As mentioned previously, everything builds on itself. Days turn to weeks, weeks turn to months and months turn to years. In the same way God's sabbatical system builds on itself. It goes like this:

• **7th Day (Sabbath)** - God rested on the seventh day. It marks rest or Sabbath.

• **7th Year (Sabbatical Year or Shemitah)** - The 7th year the land is to rest, a sabbatical year. This set of 7 is called a Shemitah.

• **7th Sabbatical Year (Jubilee Cycle)** - After 7 sets of sabbatical years there is a Jubilee Year (50th).

We know that on the 7th day of creation God rested and commanded His people to do the same, the Sabbath day. The command was also given to Moses in the 25th Chapter of Leviticus to take a Sabbatical Year (Shemitah) and Jubilee Year. It builds on itself and is intended to give people and the land they occupy rest.

Shemitah

"Six years you shall sow your field, and six years you shall prune your vineyard and gather in its crop, but during the seventh year the land shall have a sabbath rest, a sabbath to the Lord; you shall not sow your field nor prune your vineyard." - Leviticus 25:3-4

Jubilee Year

"You are also to count off seven sabbaths of years for yourself, seven times seven years, so that you have the time of the seven sabbaths of years, namely, forty-nine years. You shall then sound a ram's horn abroad on the tenth day of the seventh month; on the day of atonement you shall sound a horn all through your land. You shall thus consecrate the fiftieth year and proclaim a release through the land to all its inhabitants. It shall be a jubilee for you, and each of you shall return to his own property, and each of you shall return to his family." - Leviticus 25:8-10

Just as the Sabbath system builds on itself, so does prophecy. **This is because the entire system is Messianic. It all points to Jesus.** The theme is salvific and it points to rest in Jesus, ultimately in Heaven, in the new Zion.

A great example of telescopic prophecy is Daniel 9.

Daniel 9 is a famous passage of prophecy because it predicted with remarkable accuracy the Triumphal Entry of Christ into Jerusalem. It not only predicted the Triumphal Entry of Jesus but goes on to speak toward His Second Coming. Daniel 9, called the prophecy of the 70 Weeks is built on the Sabbatical cycle. It consists of 70 Sabbatical cycles or Shemitah years [70 sets of 7]. However there is a pause between the 69th Week and the 70th Week, representing the Time of the Gentiles prior to the final 7 year period known as the Tribulation.

This is why it is important that we set a foundation of understanding regarding the Sabbatical cycle, because everything is built on it. This way we can interpret correctly the signs correlated to the Shemitah and Jubilee Year which will help us accurately apply prophetic scripture to our day. Now that we have a foundation with God's Sabbatical system we can apply it to the passage.

What it reveals is profound.

A [Quick] History Lesson

The book of Daniel begins in 605 B.C. during the third year of Jehoiakim's reign (608-598 B.C.). Jehoiakim was appointed king by Necho II, King of Egypt, in 608 B.C. After Egypt was defeated by the Babylonians in 605 B.C. Nebuchadnezzar besieged Jerusalem, the same year that Nebuchadnezzar succeeded his father Nabopolassar as king of Babylon.

It was in 605 B.C. where select "young men of Judah's royal family and other noble families" (Daniel 1) were taken to Babylon from Judah, this is considered the first wave of deportation of the Babylonian Exile. Daniel was included in this first wave and in exile he would begin to prophesy.

After the siege Jehoiakim was forced to pay tribute to Nebuchadnezzar. This occurred until a failed Babylonian invasion of Egypt in 601 B.C. would undermine Babylonian control of Judah. Jehoiakim would then switch allegiance back to Egypt which angered Nebuchadnezzar and would lead to the Siege of Jerusalem in 597 B.C.

Jehoiakim died during the siege, he was succeeded by his son Jehoachin (or Jeconiah) who would reign only 3 months and 10 days. The Siege of Jerusalem in late 598 B.C. to 597 B.C. would lead to the second wave of deportation. In this deportation Ezekiel was taken captive to Babylon. Ezekiel would begin to prophesy in 593 B.C. He would lose is wife, as prophetically revealed to him by God [Ezekiel 24], in the 9th year of exile, when he was 34 years of age.

The final wave of deportation would occur in 582-581 B.C.

Although deportation and the exile of Judah was a process starting in 605 B.C., the marker of the formal 70 year Babylonian Exile is set from the destruction of the Temple in 586 B.C. and concludes with the rebuilding of the Second Temple in 516 B.C.

The Babylonian Exile (586-516) was a 70 year period which began with the end of the First Temple period. Jews would be in exile under Babylonian control until the fall of Babylon in 539 B.C. This would then shift to Persian control in October of 539 B.C. when Persian King Cyrus the Great would invade and conquer Babylonia, turning it into a colony of Persia. Once in power Cyrus would issue a decree known as Cyrus's Edict in 538 B.C. [Cyrus's Declaration] declaring that the Temple be rebuilt in Jerusalem (2 Chronicles 36:22-23). 10

This would begin the "Return to Zion" and the first return of exiles to Jerusalem. As a result of this decree construction would begin at the old Temple site. After a brief halt due to opposition from people who 'filled the vacuum' during Jewish captivity, the work would resume in 521 B.C. under the rule of Darius I. **It was during the first year of King Darius' reign where Daniel would receive the vision of the 70 Weeks (Daniel 9).**

Daniel 9 - The 70 Weeks

Daniel 9 opens in the first year of King Darius' reign.

After observing the Word of the Lord given to his contemporary Jeremiah about the number of years in which Jerusalem would remain desolate [70 Years - Jeremiah 29] , Daniel begins to pray and fast, confessing his sins and the sins of his people [Daniel 9:1-6]. After his prayer Daniel is met by the angel Gabriel, it is then that Daniel would receive the prophecy of the 70 Weeks.

"Seventy weeks have been decreed for your people and your holy city, to finish the transgression, to make an end of sin, to make atonement for iniquity, to bring in everlasting righteousness, to seal up vision and prophecy and to anoint the most holy place. **So you are to know and discern that from the issuing of a decree to restore and rebuild Jerusalem until Messiah the Prince there will be seven weeks and sixty-two weeks**; it will be built again, with plaza and moat, even in times of distress. **Then after the sixty-two weeks the Messiah will be cut off and have nothing, and the people of the prince who is to come will destroy the city and the sanctuary.** And its end will come with a flood; even to the end there will be war; desolations are determined. And he will make a firm covenant with the many for one week, but in the middle of the week he will put a stop to sacrifice and grain offering; and on the wing of abominations will come one who makes desolate, even until a complete destruction, one that is decreed, is poured out on the one who makes desolate." - Daniel 9:24-27 (NASB)

So what was this precise prophecy explaining?

The main prophetic implication of this passage is located in the first section, an historically accurate prediction of the Triumphal Entry of Christ into Jerusalem exactly 483 years from the proclamation of King Artaxerxes I in 445 B.C. In also goes on to predict the reconstruction and destruction of the Second Temple. But after this there is a gap in the prophecy.

It then jumps to a period known as the Tribulation, speaking of the Abomination of Desolation or when the Antichrist desecrates the Temple and gives insight into how the Tribulation will begin by covenant. It concludes by stating that the Antichrist will break the covenant half way through the 7 year period and will rule until his final destruction.

But before we address the future tense of the latter portion of Daniel 9, let's look at the already fulfilled historical application of what is often called the Daniel 9 Clock.

The Daniel 9 Clock

It was Gabriel who declared to Daniel in Chapter 9:

"So you are to know and discern that from the issuing of a decree to restore and rebuild Jerusalem until Messiah the Prince there will be seven weeks and sixty-two weeks; it will be built again, with plaza and moat, even in times of distress."
- Daniel 9:25 (NASB)

We know, in historical hindsight, that the decree mentioned in Daniel 9:25 is the command given by Artaxerxes I to Nehemiah.

In the 20th year of his reign, Artaxerxes I allowed Nehemiah (cup bearer) to return to Judah in order to restore and rebuild Jerusalem, namely the wall. Nehemiah was sent to Judah as governor of the province with a mission to rebuild. The command to "restore and rebuild Jerusalem" 11 was given by Artaxerxes I in 445 B.C. (Nehemiah 2:5-8). This was the beginning of the Daniel 9 Clock.

The "weeks" of Daniel 9 are actually sabbatical or Shemitah years. The 70 "Sevens" are actually 70 sabbatical years or 490 years in the aggregate. The total prophetic period is broken out into 3 segments:

7 Weeks (7x7) = 49 Years - Time that it took to rebuild Jerusalem. Chronicled by the Book of Nehemiah.

62 Weeks (62x7) = 434 Years - Using the Jewish 360 day calendar, this period of time is to be added with the 49 years mentioned above to gain an aggregate. It gives us 483 years (49+434). 483 years after Artaxerxes I proclamation in 445 B.C. places us at A.D. 30 or the Triumphal Entry of Christ.

1 Week (7) = Final Week or Tribulation

With amazing historical accuracy the first portion of the 70 Weeks prophecy predicts from the proclamation of Artaxerxes I the Triumphal Entry of Christ into Jerusalem. Yet following this we have a gap, this gap in Daniel's prophecy stands between the death of Christ and the destruction of the Second Temple to the covenant marking the Tribulation or final "week".

Why is that?

It is because it represents the period of time following the destruction of the Temple in 70 A.D. (which Jesus also prophesied) until the final restoration of Israel before the Tribulation. This period of time is known as the Time of the Gentiles, as spoken by Jesus in the Olivet Discourse as documented by Luke.

Mind the Gap

The gap between the 69th week and the 70th week of Daniel's prophecy marks the exile of Jews after the rejection of the Messiah and the destruction of the Second Temple in 70 A.D. It spans a period of time which concludes when the Jews are placed back in their land prior to the Tribulation [Ezekiel 37-39].

There is a reason why Ezekiel was taken in the second wave of deportation after Daniel. The reason being that his prophecies fill the gap, they speak to the restoration of the Jewish people after their dispersion related to the rejection of the Messiah, after the Siege of Jerusalem [70 A.D.]. Once this regathering is complete the final week of Daniel's prophecy commences, which is the Tribulation, and Daniel's prophecy carries on.

Daniel receives the vision of the 70 Weeks while observing the writings of Jeremiah's 70 year prophecy also for a reason. Because Daniel was the next step after Jeremiah's prophecy. Daniel would prophesy and then the gap in his prophecy was to be prophesied by Ezekiel, who came behind Daniel literally in the deportation. Like the Sabbatical system, prophecy and even the works of the prophets all builds on itself.

The gap in Daniel 9 is important because it represents the period of time in which we live. Not only do we live in this gap but signs have emerged, such as the restoration of Israel in 1948 after World War II, that we are living towards the end of this gap. Because of this the prophecies of Ezekiel are extremely important to our generation.

Remember how we addressed at the beginning of the chapter the telescopic nature of prophecy? God builds everything on cycles. Similar to how days become weeks, weeks become months and months become years; God's sabbatical cycle builds from the 7th day (Sabbath), to the 7th year (Shemitah) to 7 sets of 7 years (Jubilee).

Just as Daniel 9 was built on the Shemitah cycle, Ezekiel's prophecy was speaking to the next cycle, the Jubilee Year. His latter prophecies are about the final return of the Jews to the Promised Land before the Tribulation.

This is important, because Jubilee has not been celebrated since the first exile of Jews from the Northern Kingdom of Israel (Assyrian Exile 740-722 B.C.). In order for Jubilee to be restored all tribes must be living in the land. **Returning to**

the land is an important component of the Jubilee. So once Ezekiel's prophecy is fulfilled the Jews will once again celebrate Jubilee.

Because the prophecy of Ezekiel speaks to the time in which we live we want to pay particular attention to what it says and understand it the best we can. In the next chapters we will look at Ezekiel's prophecy and the implications it has for our day.

CHAPTER 5

THE EZEKIEL WINDOW

"In Israel, in order to be a realist you must believe in miracles." -
David Ben Gurion

Although the previous chapters may have been a little dry, the history of how we got to where we are today is important. Our history is important because it points to our future. Biblical prophecy is built on the past, for that which will happen in the future is bringing closure to what has occurred in the past, issuing us into a new era. Since God built everything on Sabbatical cycles we know that prophecy is built on them as well.

When looking at the prophecy of Daniel 9 we are amazed to see such an historically accurate and calculated prediction. We also know that the prophecies of his contemporaries such as Jeremiah and Ezekiel were precise and true. Since the prophecies fulfilled in the past were accurate, why would we expect anything less from their prophecies surrounding the future?

Since Ezekiel's prophecies fill the gap between the destruction of the Second Temple through the Time of the Gentiles and up to the Tribulation it is important that we give special attention to this vision God gave him, for it covers the time period in which we live.

You will notice that this book is building towards something.

We looked at the "Big Picture" of World War I and World War II to show their correlation to the regathering and restoration of Israel. From there we went even further back to reveal the "Bigger Picture", which are the historical cycles of Jewish exile and return. Specifically we looked at Daniel 9 and the amazing accuracy in which it predicted the Triumphal Entry of Christ. We also looked at how Ezekiel bridges the gap in Daniel's prophecy leading us up to today. We have seen supernatural accuracy in both accounts.

The book is building towards a climax because we are following the path which God set through the prophets. Just as days turn to weeks, which turn into months and years; just as sabbaths turn into Sabbatical years which turn into Jubilee years, the prophecies of God are ultimately building toward His return.

We are now faced with the question of how these prophecies apply to us today.

The Time of the Gentiles

We live in what is called the "Time of the Gentiles", it is also known as the "Church Age". Jesus addressed this in the Olivet Discourse as documented by Luke:

"...and Jerusalem will be trampled under foot by the Gentiles until the times of the Gentiles are fulfilled" - Luke 21:24 (NASB)

So this pause in Daniel 9 if two fold.

First, it is reserved for the Holy Spirit to do His work amongst the Gentiles, this is due to the rejection of the Messiah by the Jews. Second, it is a pause centered around the exile of modern day Jews after 70 A.D.

Where we gain clarity into the application of Ezekiel's prophecy regarding the Last Days is to remember that it was intended specifically for the Jews. Ultimately the prophecy of Ezekiel is just building on the prophecies of Jeremiah and Daniel, which were specifically directed towards the Jews. Keeping within that mindset we will see that any events correlated to the Shemitah or Jubilee are not about the Church, Gentiles in general or non-believing pagans, rather it is a sign for Jews living under the Law. It is entirely correlated to the Jews, the bride of the Father.

We in Christendom forget that before the Bride of Christ [Church] the Jews were the Bride of the Father. We see this in symbolism portrayed through the Book of Hosea, where the prophet Hosea was told to marry the prostitute Gomer in order to represent how God's people, the Jews, had been unfaithful in their covenant to Him. Just as the relationship of the Church to Jesus is a bride & groom relationship, the same is true about the Jews to YHWH, God the Father, who led them out of Egypt, through the desert and into the Promised Land.

It would humble the Christian to remember that we have been grafted into this family tree. That salvation was possible before Christ's physical Advent, because Abraham, Moses,

David and many others had 'faith that was credited to them as righteousness'. Before the physical coming of Jesus, the Word among us, faith in the Father was faith in the Triune Godhead, which included Jesus. This means that God is not finished with Israel. He has not only restored them as one nation [1948], but in Ezekiel we are given insight into their spiritual restoration during the Last Days.

Now that Jesus has come, salvation is only possible through faith in Him. The only way to the Father is through the Son.

"Jesus said to him, "I am the way, and the truth, and the life. No one comes to the Father except through me." - John 14:6

Jesus is going to do an amazing work of salvation among the Jewish people in the days to come. They will realize that Jesus is in fact the Messiah!

"And I will give you a new heart, and a new spirit I will put within you. And I will remove the heart of stone from your flesh and give you a heart of flesh." - Ezekiel 36:26

This passage is frequently misused by Christians and applied only to Gentile salvation. Yes, during the salvation process God gives our dead, unregenerate heart a spiritual transplant. You are given a new heart through which the Holy Spirit seals you to the Day of Redemption. However, in context this passage in Ezekiel was specifically directed to the Jewish people. It represents salvation during the latter days. A period of prophetic fulfillment, restoration and regathering where Jews will be saved by believing in the Messiah, Yeshua [Jesus], and will receive a new heart of flesh, the Spirit of God within them. The restoration begins physically but is ultimately just a foreshadowing of spiritual rebirth.

Roots: The Way

Before this Jesus following movement became known as "Christian" they were merely Jews that believed in Jesus as the Messiah. The Way, as it was called, were at first Jews that believed in Yeshua as the Messiah.

The same occurs in the Last Days, Jews begin to believe in Yeshua [Jesus] as the Messiah. We are seeing this today. Through Concept Church, the digital ministry I have the privilege of stewarding, I am connected with the organization One For Israel. Through social media and other outlets Jews are placing their faith in Yeshua in record numbers. This is why Concept Church will be focused on assisting One For Israel and their outreach to Jews in Israel. Because Ezekiel's prophecies are coming to pass today, the future is now, and technology is helping us fulfill the mission.

What we want to address in this chapter is what I call the "Ezekiel 37-39 Window". This is a period of time which speaks to the return of the Jews to their homeland. Its also predicts a large scale war in the Middle East which precedes the Tribulation. Since we have seen the regathering of Israel in 1948 we should be aware of these passages. Even more so because we are approaching significant anniversaries.

The Aliyah Awakening

Prior to 1948 and the formation of the State of Israel by the United Nations it was hard to see these prophetic passages of scripture as relevant. Prior to World War I the land of Israel was occupied by the Ottoman Empire. Even through the Mandate Palestine period after World War I, the notion of a regathered and restored Israel seemed unlikely suggesting an 'end of days' Israel to be a misinterpretation of scripture. Because of this, Christian theologians at the time reasoned that God had rejected the Jews as a result of them rejecting the Messiah, that the Church had become the new 'Israel'. There is only one problem, that isn't Biblical nor is it in line with the character of God. **He made an everlasting covenant with Abraham and that covenant involved the land.**

In Genesis we see that the land God gave them would be an **everlasting possession**.

"I will give to you and to your descendants after you, the land of your sojournings, all the land of Canaan, for an everlasting possession; and I will be their God." - Genesis 17:8 (NASB)

But the land is technically God's land. The Jews are merely stewards, as we see in the Leviticus, the passage regarding the Sabbatical system.

"The land shall not be sold in perpetuity, for the land is mine. For you are strangers and sojourners with me." - Leviticus 25:23

So if the land is an everlasting possession, why would the Jewish people be uprooted from the land? Why would they be sent into exile?

It is due to disobedience, which is mentioned in the Leviticus 26, the chapter directly following the passage regarding the Sabbatical system.

"And **I will lay your cities waste and will make your sanctuaries desolate**, and I will not smell your pleasing aromas. And I myself will devastate the land, so that your enemies who settle in it shall be appalled at it. And **I will scatter you among the nations**, and I will unsheathe the sword after you, and your land shall be a desolation, and your cities shall be a waste." - Leviticus 26:31-33

So the exile of the Jewish people through the Assyrian & Babylonian Captivity, the destruction of the First and Second Temple and the exile of current day diaspora Jews **was in direct fulfillment of God's Word to the Jewish people regarding disobedience and Sabbatical system observance**. This is why the Shemitah and Jubilee Year are so important to our day. Because if God is restoring them physically, He intends to do so spiritually. It is a marker of the Last Days.

After a period of discipline and exile in accordance to the Law based on their iniquity, God would do as He had promised which was to restore and renew His chosen people, something we have seen in our lifetime. The theological perspective regarding Israel would change after World War II. After 1948 with the State of Israel now an official, sovereign nation acknowledged by the United Nations, the evidence was among us that God was beginning His final work, a sign that we are in the final stages of the Time of the Gentiles.

We are currently in a period called Aliyah, which is the immigration of Jews moving from diaspora to the land of Israel. Also defined as the act of "going up" to Jerusalem, it is a basic tenet of Zionism. Under the Law of Return, a piece of Israeli legislation passed on July 5, 1950, Jews were given the right to return and live in Israel to gain Israeli citizenship. In 1970 this was extended to people with one Jewish grandparent or people married to a Jew.

In 2014 Aliyah saw record breaking numbers as a result of anti-semitism in Europe and around the world. That year Israel saw over 26,500 immigrants participate which was a 32% increase from 2013. There was also a 7% increase in people immigrating from the US, Canada and the UK. But the number just keeps growing. At the end of 2015 the estimated number was more than 30,000 Jews immigrating to Israel. Another 16% increase from the previous year. 12

It was as Ezekiel prophesied:

"Behold, **I will take the sons of Israel from among the nations where they have gone, and I will gather them** from every side and bring them into their own land; **and I will make them one nation in the land,** on the mountains of Israel; and one king will be king for all of them; and **they will no longer be two nations and no longer be divided into two kingdoms.**" - Ezekiel 37:21-22

The nation is one and the Jewish people are coming home.

The Kingdom, United

What is so miraculous is not just that the Nation of Israel was restored but also that the Kingdom is no longer divided. This is an extremely important piece of the fulfillment. Israel in the north and Judah in the south are now one nation, the Nation of Israel. Prior to the Assyrian Exile [740-722 B.C.] the Jewish people were divided but now they are one. The implications are enormous. Why? **Because they are now ready for Jubilee.**

Full Circle - The 10 Lost Tribes

There were 12 tribes that originally settled and took possession of the land of Canaan, the Promised Land. They were as follows:

Asher, Dan, Joseph (Ephraim & Manasseh), Gad, Issachar, Naphtali, Reuben, Simeon, Zebulun, Levi, Benjamin and Judah.

In 930 B.C. 10 tribes would form the independent Kingdom of Israel in the north while tribes of Judah and Benjamin would set up the Kingdom of Judah in the south. The Jewish people were divided. However it was the conquest of the Northern Kingdom of Israel by the Assyrians in 740 B.C. which resulted in the 10 northern tribes being assimilated by other peoples. This is called the Ten Lost Tribes of Israel. It was during this time that the Jubilee ceased being observed, for it requires all tribes living in the land.

Here is some insight from Rabbi Baruch S. Davidson regarding the Jubilee.

"According to biblical law, the Jubilee is only observed when all twelve tribes of the Jewish nation are living in Israel, as is derived from the verse, "And you shall sanctify the fiftieth year, and proclaim freedom throughout the land for all who live on it," which implies that the Jubilee is only sanctified when "all who live on it"—meaning, all who are meant to be living there—are in the Land of Israel. Furthermore, the Jubilee is only observed when every tribe is living in the specific part of the land which was it was allotted when the Land of Israel was divided. However, some are of the opinion that the Jubilee is observed as long as there is a partial representation of each tribe, even if most of the tribe is not in Israel.

In the 6th century BCE, the Assyrians conquered the Northern Kingdom of Israel and sent the majority of its population into exile. Those who were deported are historically known as the Ten Lost Tribes.

We are certain that before that point in time the Jubilee was regularly observed. We also know that, with the destruction of the Second Temple and the disbandment of the Sanhedrin (supreme rabbinical court), we ceased to mark the Jubilee year in any form. The periods about which there is a question are the remaining years between the exile of the Ten Tribes and the destruction of the First Temple, and the Second Temple Era.

According to the opinion that partial representation of each tribe is sufficient to fulfill the scriptural requirement, biblically mandated Jubilees were fully observed throughout the periods in question, because there remained a small representation of each tribe in Israel.

However, according to the first opinion mentioned above, with the exile of the Northern Kingdom the required condition for the Jubilee to be sanctified was lost. Thus, the last time there was a biblical requirement to observe the Jubilee was about 150 years before the destruction of the First Temple.

The question remains, however, whether according to this opinion Jubilee years were designated or observed during this time by rabbinic injunction. This is the subject of debate amongst the sages.

As mentioned above, though, today the Jubilee year is neither designated nor observed.

And now for the answer to your question: "When is the next Jubilee year?"

We eagerly await the day when G-d will bring our

entire nation back to our homeland—including the ten "lost" tribes—and we will again resume observing the Jubilee year, as well as so many other mitzvot which we are incapable of performing until that awaited day." - Rabbi Baruch S. Davidson 13

They might as well the get the good wine ready for the mitzvot because all signs point to a Jubilee in their future. However, they will also face great trial and tribulation as we near the end of the gap in Daniel 9. **God is bringing them together as one for a reason, because they will have to stand together and fight against the world.** But before the Tribulation commences, the end of the restoration and regathering period concludes with a great war. This great war is documented in Ezekiel 38 and 39 and is known as the Gog and Magog War, or Ezekiel's Magog.

Understanding Ezekiel's prophecy about Magog is of paramount importance today. Why?

Because we are approaching the 70th anniversary of the State of Israel in 2018. That same year we will celebrate the 100 year anniversary of the end of World War I, the war which repossessed the Holy Land and began the entire restoration process for Israel.

Even as I write this, the prophesied Magog nations are gaining strategic momentum north of Israel and war appears on the horizon just as we enter this strategic period of time. A time marked with anniversaries that signify the completion or closure of an event based on a Biblical generation, which is something I will explain in more detail later.

Signs are emerging that point to further fulfillment of Ezekiel's prophecy.

Ezekiel's prophecy is about large scale completion of the Time of the Gentiles concluding with the restoration and regathering of the Nation of Israel, all 12 tribes. Since the Jubilee system was stopped with the fall of the Northern Kingdom, the completion of this prophecy will bring about the following:

- All tribes living in the land.
- The prophesied Third Temple [Ezekiel's Temple].
- The restoration of Jubilee Year observance.

The Decree of Cyrus after the Babylonian Exile was similar to the United Nations' declaration of the State of Israel. **Both marked the beginning of a rebuilding period.** As the decree of Cyrus led to the rebuilding of Jerusalem and the Temple, the decree set forth by the United Nations is rebuilding Israel and will ultimately lead to the third and final Temple being constructed, as prophesied by Ezekiel.

However before we get there, there is a large war in the Middle East as prophesied in Ezekiel 38-39. This war brings closure to the gap in Daniel 9, the Time of the Gentiles, and leads us into the Tribulation. Evidence of this war is building today. Regarding this 'Magog' war we need to answer the following questions:

• What is Magog?

• What signs should we look for?

• Is recent military build up in the Middle East a sign that this war is on the horizon?

• Who is involved in this war?

• What is the outcome?

We will go over all of this in the next chapter.

CHAPTER 6

THE FINAL WARS

"You may have to fight a battle more than once to win it." -
Margaret Thatcher

We have been at war since before creation. As you read through scripture you will notice a central theme of war. Throughout scripture there is a common theme of the Kingdom of God vs the anti-kingdom, the kingdom of Satan. It is a battle of light vs darkness, good vs evil and life vs death. This war has been waged since Lucifer's rebellion and subsequent fall.

But it was in the Garden of Eden where mankind was brought into the fight. It was there where man, like Lucifer, would fall.

After Satan infiltrated the Garden he manipulated the heart of man and as a result caused the fruit or manifestation of the anti-kingdom in man. It was at this point where the war in the spiritual realm would manifest itself in the physical. Man would war against man.

Satan did not have to kill us, he would just have to set us against each other and we would kill ourselves.

We first see this in the murder of Abel by his brother Cain. In a fit of jealousy and rage, even after rebuke from

God, Cain would kill his brother Abel. Because of this he would be sent into the wilderness to wander. But in disobedience he would settle in the land of Nod and as a result, wickedness would breed and eventually take over the earth until one day God had enough and decided to start over again. This would lead to the Great Flood and the story of Noah, his 3 sons Shem, Ham, Japheth and their wives.

However, even after God went to great lengths to destroy wicked men the flood did not cure the wicked heart of man. The cycle of depravity would start all over again. Known as the "Generations of Noah" or the "Table of Nations", all three sons would go on to populate the world as we know it today. Ham would settle Canaan, the Sinai peninsula and Northern Africa. Shem would settle the Arabian peninsula and Mesopotamia while Japheth would settle Asia Minor and to the west, into what is now modern day Europe.

Of particular importance, at least for the sake of this chapter, is the line of Japheth, where the descendants of Japheth settled and what that means for today.

The Bloodline

To understand Magog you first have to understand the bloodline. If you are like me you are probably quick to skip over genealogies in the Bible. They seem mundane and unimportant. For a period of time when I was reading through the Bible I would see a long genealogy and think, "Oh nice, I can just skip over this section!". However these sections of scripture are extremely important and they are there for a reason.

It is well known the importance of the Davidic line, this lineage helps us to track and validate prophecies related to Christ, but other genealogies are important because they help give clarity into how certain people groups settled different regions. It all started after the flood with the sons of Noah. His bloodline helps us understand cultures, civilizations and future prophecy better.

To track Magog we need to look at Noah's bloodline through his son Japheth. Noah's son Japheth would end up fathering 7 sons: Gomer, Magog, Madai, Javan, Tubal, Meshech, and Tiras. Their descendants would continue settling in the area to the north and west of Israel. After Babel they would go on to speak what are classified today as the Indo-European languages.

It was Japheth's descendants that would settle in the region known as "Magog" in Ezekiel's prophecy.

But Magog isn't just a person or a people group that settled the region north of Israel. The term has a spiritual meaning which is mentioned in Ezekiel 38 & 39 as well as in Revelation 20. In context it speaks to a 'united nations' against Israel in the Last Days. So to understand Magog fully we want to take both the literal and historic meaning and apply it to the prophetic.

Understanding Magog

To have a full understanding of Magog we have to look at it from a literal and historical sense as well as from a spiritual and prophetic sense. All work together to give us a complete picture. Here is a synopsis or breakdown of Magog on all three levels. Magog is the following:

1. A person, the grandson of Noah, the second son of Japheth.

2. A people group. Magog's descendants would end up settling the area north of Israel, which is Asia Minor or the area known as modern day Turkey. They would go on to settle the area north of the Black Sea (Russia) as well as modern day Europe.

3. In prophecy Magog represents the uniting of nations against Israel. In Ezekiel Magog has specific regional significance with a specified list of nations. In the Book of Revelation Magog is the final war, commonly referred to as Armageddon, which includes all nations.

So to make the rest of this chapter easier to grasp, when we are speaking of "Magog" we are speaking of it in the prophetical sense as defined by Ezekiel.

Although the staging ground for Ezekiel's Magog, the war prior to the Tribulation, is in literal Asia Minor (the land settled by the descendants of Japheth's son Magog) in the Book of Revelation Magog is a 'united nations' against the elect for the final battle, what is commonly referred to as

Armageddon. Gog and Magog represent a group of nations and a leader, Gog, who leads these nations against Israel.

In short, Magog in prophecy is the uniting of nations against God and His people. It starts regionally, around Israel, then spreads around the world. So who is Gog?

Gog represents both a physical and spiritual power. In Ezekiel, Gog (Rosh) is a world leader who leads the initial consortium of nations. This world leader is not to be confused with the Antichrist. The Antichrist emerges after the war to diplomatically restore peace and broker a covenant (Daniel 9) with Israel and the Magog nations.

In the Book of Revelation Gog is also the leader of Magog but at this point Magog has grown to include all the nations of the world and is led by Satan himself.

Ezekiel's Magog War

This may be my favorite chapter of the book because it shines so much light on what we are seeing in our generation. It brings clarity and perspective to the conditions of the world geopolitically, specifically to what may be setting up in the Middle East even as I write this book.

The entire book has been building up to this moment. We want to answer the following questions.

• Do we live in prophetic times?
• Can we accurately apply scripture to our day and see the implications of prophetic fulfillment around us?

• If so, what should we look for?

The answer is yes, to all of the above. We are living in prophetic times and we can apply the scriptures accurately to our day. But in order to know what to look for you have to accurately interpret the text. Now that we have the historical background work done we can dig in to the modern day application.

Details of the War

This first Magog War (Gog and Magog) is detailed in Ezekiel 38 & 39. The passage is titled "The Prophecy of Magog and the Future Invasion of Israel", and it reads:

"Therefore prophesy, son of man, and say to Gog, 'Thus says the Lord God, "**On that day when my people Israel are living securely**, will you not know it? **You will come from your place out of the remote parts of the north, you and many peoples with you,** all of them riding on horses, a great assembly and a mighty army; and you will come up against my people Israel like a cloud to cover the land. It shall come about in the last days that I will bring you against my land, so that the nations may know me when I am sanctified through you before their eyes, O Gog." - Ezekiel 38:14-16 (NASB)

Following sequentially after Ezekiel 37, chapters 38 & 39 speak to this leader, Gog, bringing a specified group of nations against Israel, along with a great assembly of others after Israel has been regathered and restored living securely in the land (v.14).

"After many days you will be mustered. **In the latter years you will go against the land that is restored from war, the land whose people were gathered from many peoples upon the mountains of Israel**, which had been a continual waste. Its people were brought out from the peoples and now dwell securely, all of them." - Ezekiel 38:8 (NASB)

The war is particularly devastating.

"But on that day, the day that Gog shall come against the land of Israel, declares the Lord God, my wrath will be roused in my anger. **For in my jealousy and in my blazing wrath I declare, on that day there shall be a great earthquake in the land of Israel.** The fish of the sea and the birds of the heavens and the beasts of the field and all creeping things that creep on the ground, and all the people who are on the face of the earth, shall quake at my presence. And the mountains shall be thrown down, and the cliffs shall fall, and every wall shall tumble to the ground. I will summon a sword against Gog on all my mountains, declares the Lord God. Every man's sword will be against his brother. With pestilence and bloodshed I will enter into judgment with him, **and I will rain upon him and his hordes and the many peoples who are with him torrential rains and hailstones, fire and sulfur.** " - Ezekiel 38:18-22

God releases severe judgement on the nations trying to undo what He has done, which is the restoration of Israel. There is an earthquake and significant fallout in the northern hills or mountains of Israel. Modern day interpretation of "fire and sulfur" raining down interpret the passage as a significant military weapon such as a nuclear weapon or WMD used against Gog and Magog.

Literalists believe it could be a supernatural act of God, like that of Sodom and Gomorrah. Whatever the case may be, the judgement is so severe that the fall out lasts for 7 years.

"Then those who dwell in the cities of Israel will go out and make fires of the weapons and burn them, shields and bucklers, bow and arrows, clubs and spears; **and they will make fires of them for seven years**, so that they will not need to take wood out of the field or cut down any out of the forests, **for they will make their fires of the weapons.** They will seize the spoil of those who despoiled them, and plunder those who plundered them, declares the Lord God." - Ezekiel 39:9-10

Obviously we do not use "shields and bucklers, bows and arrows, clubs and spears" anymore today. This is why it is important to not take everything in prophecy literally, for much of it is symbolism. In many of the visions God gave to the prophets He would use images contemporary to their day in order to explain future and forward things. Since they had not seen the weaponry or technology we have today, it could only be explained using objects they would have known and it can sometimes create obscure imagery.

We see the use of such symbolism in Ezekiel 39:9. It is less about the fallout of war, although significant and a sign that the war is severe, but rather the terminology used is a reference point of time and placement. Israel using the cache of weapons as a source of fuel for 7 years is symbolic and places the war directly before the 7 year Tribulation. This separates Ezekiel's Magog War from the Gog and Magog War of Revelation.

It is in this passage where we can see the connection between the closure of the Time of the Gentiles, or the pause in Daniel 9, and the beginning of the 7 year period of the Tribulation. It is after this devastating war that the Antichrist emerges and uses diplomacy as a means to bring about long awaited peace in the Middle East.

Nuclear Implications

It is because of the symbolic nature of Ezekiel 39:9-10 where I am inclined to view the judgement unleashed on Magog in Ezekiel 38:18-22 as that of a nuclear weapon or WMD. Much of the prophetic vision given to Ezekiel and John on the Island of Patmos [Book of Revelation] was given using imagery that they would have known [animals, current day military application, etc]. The context of application was far beyond what they knew. Or actual images were given in the vision, for example to John in the Revelation, and they could only be explained combining elements he knew, which creates obscure imagery for us today.

Although the use of nuclear weapons or other WMD by Israel would be severe it would be in line with the passage. A strike with dual meaning: that the people of Israel will not have their sovereignty questioned or challenged, also the unleashing of God's judgement against those who are trying to undo what the World Wars accomplished.

But this is not based on a hunch, rather the result of connection. The reason being the connection between World War I and World War II as we discussed in Chapter 3, the "Big Picture". It is all about how World War II ended.

Not only was World War I the beginning of Ezekiel 37, since it repossessed the Holy Land (Palestine) from the Ottoman Empire, but this repossession occurred towards the end of the war. It would then set up World War II. Once World War II was complete, Mandate Palestine would then be turned over to the newly formed United Nations and the land would be partitioned, giving birth to the State of Israel.

You have to pay attention to how both wars ended.

Just as how the way World War I ended was a set up for World Word II, the way World War II ended is a set up for the next world wide engagement, which we know could be Ezekiel's Magog War.

World War II ended with a nuclear bomb and sets the stage for the next war. It will be severe and because of the correlation to World War II the nuclear bomb will likely be used during or to bring about closure to World War III, Ezekiel's Magog War. This is also in line with the text.

"...and I will rain upon him and his hordes and the many peoples who are with him torrential rains and hailstones, fire and sulfur." - Ezekiel 38:22

As World War II ended with the statehood of Israel, it sets the stage for that statehood to be challenged in the next world wide engagement. Any attempt to undo what has been done will be met with severe consequences, whatever they may be, whether man-made or supernatural intervention from God.

Putting the Puzzle Pieces Together

In Ezekiel's prophecy, what I call the Ezekiel Window, the nation of Israel is restored from war and regathered when the prophesied invasion will occur. In contrast to Armageddon, Ezekiel's Magog occurs before the Tribulation and completes the "Time of the Gentiles" ushering us into to the final week of Daniel's prophecy in Chapter 9, the 70 Weeks.

This is why the repossession of the Holy Land as a result of World War I was so significant. Also why the formation of the State of Israel in 1948 after World War II was equally significant. It is because we witnessed the repossession of the Holy Land and the rebirth of Israel.

This rebirth was both historic and symbolic. Historic in that it literally fulfilled the prophecy surrounding Israel in the Last Days, a kingdom restored as one and not divided between north and south. Also a symbolic restoration which speaks of a period of time where many Jews will come to salvation through faith in Yeshua [Jesus], the Messiah.

Israel is now securely living in the land as prophesied in Ezekiel 37 for the first time since 70 A.D. and the destruction of the Second Temple. Within one Biblical generation (100 years) we have seen both the repossession of the Holy Land, the regathering of Jews from diaspora exile and the resettlement of Israel as a single, unified nation, bringing to completion what was prophesied in Ezekiel 37.

Not only was Israel unified as a single nation, the world was unified as well.

The birth of the United Nations after World War II would set into motion the beginning of the unified world. The emergence of a nuclear weapon at the end of WWII would force the need for a more centralized, global diplomacy. But the implications of a restored Israel just sets the stage for greater, prophetic fulfillment.

The Third Temple

As we approach 2018 [the 100 year anniversary of World War I and the 70 year anniversary of the State of Israel] we come into a period which should be ripe for Biblical fulfillment. The reason being that these are generational markers which God has, in history, used to mark completion and prophetic fulfillment, specifically as it relates to the Temple.

• We see this with David, whom was not allowed to build the First Temple because of the blood on his hands from war. As a result, the task would be given to the next generation, Solomon's generation. David would live exactly 70 years, which was a generation or the life of a king as set forth in scripture.

• We also see this in the Babylonian Exile. Where as Jeremiah prophesied, the Israelites would remain in exile for 70 years before returning to the land. This happened exactly as Jeremiah prophesied, the Jews would return exactly 70 years later as marked by the period of time which spanned the destruction of the First Temple and the beginning of construction on the Second Temple.

• Again we see this through the birth of Christ, where within 70 years of the birth of Christ, the life of a king, the prophesied destruction of the Second Temple would occur in 70 A.D.

The implications for today are this: that we are living in the 70 year period after 1948. This generational period completes itself in 2018. Also in 2018 is the 100 year anniversary of World War I, or the generational marker completing the entire Ezekiel 37 process. Both of the these generational markers point to the completion of Ezekiel 37 and the beginning of the Temple reconstruction period.

In scripture a generation is defined in three ways: 40 years, 70 years [the life of a king] and 100 years. But in this case a 70 year generation is of importance, due to its historical correlation to the Temple.

As we see in the examples above, the generational marker of completion as it correlates to the Temple is 70 years.

1. David must die [70] before Solomon can build the First Temple.
2. Regarding the Babylonian Captivity, the Israelites must

be in exile for 70 years (marked by the destruction of the First Temple) before the reconstruction of the Second Temple may commence.

3. The Second Temple was not destroyed until 70 years after the birth of the King of Kings, Jesus.

In all these cases, a 70 year generation must be complete before what is prophesied about the Temple may occur, be that destruction or construction.

The birth of the State of Israel began a special clock. Just as the Jews would return from Babylon 70 years later as defined by Temple construction, just as the Second Temple would be destroyed within 70 years of Jesus' birth, this clock surrounds the Temple. The fact that we are almost 70 years from the rebirth of Israel is important.

As we approach the 70 year anniversary of the State of Israel, their restoration and regathering after World War II, it means that we are entering into a period of Temple reconstruction as defined by Biblical, historical trend. The necessary generation of 70 years, marked by the life of a king, which is needed between one act of fulfillment to the next, will be complete and the historical significance is correlated to the Temple. All of these converge in 2018, which means we are entering a transitory period, where we are ripe for Biblical fulfillment.

If this is true it means Ezekiel's Magog War is around the corner. So how do we apply the text regarding Magog in scripture to the nations today?

Ezekiel's Magog Today

As we stated in the beginning of the chapter, Magog is a person, the grandson of Noah, the second son of Japheth. Magog's descendants would end up settling a region of the earth, specifically Asia Minor and even further north into the Black Sea region. But spiritually and prophetically speaking, Magog is a "united nations" against Israel. It starts in Ezekiel and builds toward ultimate climax in Revelation.

The coalition begins regionally and the nations involved are as follows:

Rosh, Magog, Meshech, Tubal, Persia, Cush, Gomer and Beth-togarmah.

Based on the Table of Nations and the settlement of Japheth's descendants in conjunction with Revelation 2, we can know the location of Ezekiel's Magog as it correlates to todays sovereign representation.

Magog in Ezekiel 38 & 39 is the region of Asia Minor or modern day Turkey. This is the staging ground for the war as it comes down on Israel from the North. But other nations are involved and come together. They include:

Gog (or Rosh) = **Russia**

Magog = **Turkey**

Meshech & Tubal = **Turkey & Georgia**

Gomer & Beth-togarmah = **Turkey**

Persia = **Iran**

Put = **Libya**

Cush = **Ethiopia or Sudan**

These are the nations that will come together, in the final stages of the regathering and restoration of Israel, to wage war against Israel. The nations listed above in modern day terminology should sound familiar, because they are all in the news today. We are seeing this consortium starting to emerge in the Middle East and it is happening with impeccable timing.

Bringing it All Together

Since 1948 the rise of Dispensationalism has had a large impact on eschatology. Primarily because of the emergence of the State of Israel, which gave illumination to scripture and allowed us to see how Israel would exist in conjunction with the Church in the Last Days. However not everything that came from this was beneficial, it has also led to many misapplications. One example being the widely held belief that Russia is Magog and its leader would be the Gog or Rosh mentioned in Ezekiel. Although it could be correlated that Rosh, which represents a people north of the Black Sea, is the leader of Magog, an overemphasis was placed on Russia due to the Cold War coinciding with the height of Dispensationalism in America, especially during the 1980's.

It is also due to a misunderstanding of the migration of the Scythian people. Many look at the time period of the historian Josephus to place the Scythians north of the Black Sea. However, at the time when Ezekiel would prophesy regarding Magog this people group would've been located in Asia Minor, or modern day Turkey.

The Scythians represent modern day Ukraine, Southern Russia and Crimea and they were master's of mounted warfare. But at large, this "Gog and Magog" area in Ezekiel is the area around the Black Sea and into Asia Minor or modern day Turkey. It also includes Iran and areas of northern Africa.

Those names should ring a bell.

You may recall the 2011 Arab Spring uprising and revolution in Libya which led to the ousting of President Gaddafi and the well known incident at the US diplomatic compound in Benghazi. A nation prophesied to be a part of this movement against Israel. It is also interesting that Egypt, Syria and Iraq are not included in the list of Ezekiel's Magog. Both Syria and Iraq are in states of decay. Internal fighting and civil war have left Syria a wasteland. After the withdrawal of US troops from Iraq, ISIS (or ISIL) has emerged in the region and seeks take back land and restore the Caliphate of the Ottoman Empire. A caliphate that directly violates the sovereignty of Turkey.

Russia, which now occupies Georgia, Crimea and Eastern Ukraine has carved a path down through the Black Sea and recently placed military operations in Syria. Even though Russian forces have been withdrawn due to frustration with

Iran, it is likely to be temporary as Vladimir Putin has stated continued support for Assad and that he could redeploy forces within hours. All of this as Turkey (remnants of the old Ottoman Empire) are seeking to invade Syria to the south in order to defend its sovereignty against ISIL, which occupies the southeast portion of Syria.

Even though what is happening in the Middle East is a moving target, what is happening in the aggregate has all the signs that Ezekiel's prophecy is coming together. The nations of Magog, prophesied by Ezekiel, are emerging. The players are moving into the region and it appears to be occurring with perfect timing.

But what does this mean for the Church?

Before we can move forward with modern day analysis and practical application we have to look at a famous passage of scripture regarding the end. It is from Jesus Himself. What I am referring to is the Olivet Discourse and we will look at it in the next chapter.

CHAPTER 7

THE DISCOURSE

"My concern is not whether God is on our side; my greatest concern is to be on God's side, for God is always right." - Abraham Lincoln

God is always right and He is always on time. When you look back at history you will see a faithful God. You will also see His perfect timing. Whether it was the prophecy surrounding the Babylonian Exile, the subsequent return of the Jews 70 years later, the rebuilding of the Second Temple, the Triumphal Entry of Christ or the Fall of Jerusalem in 70 A.D., we see that God has perfect timing. He is the same both yesterday, today and forever. Because of this we know that future events will transpire with perfect timing as well.

As I was reading through scripture and studying how prophecy transpired over the years the thought occurred to me, "If the Bible is all about Jesus, then what He said about His return should be the plumb line to which all end times prophecy is compared against."

What I am referring to is called the Olivet Discourse. The passage is most often quoted from Matthew 24 but it is also located in Mark 13 and Luke 21.

I came to this dilemma while writing the book: Ezekiel's Magog precedes the "final week" of Daniel 9 which leads us into the Tribulation. But in mainstream Christianity Pre-Tribulation rapture is a widely held belief. In the past I would tend to stay away from the topic of the rapture because it is so controversial. But this crossroads forced me to dig into scripture and see what the text had to say about the matter. To diligently seek what Jesus had to say about His own return and to use it as the plumb line for which all "Last Days" scripture should be tested.

I needed to answer the following questions:

• What did Jesus say about His return?
• How does what Jesus say sync with other passages in scripture from Revelation, to the prophets (Jeremiah, Daniel and Ezekiel) and the writings of Paul to the Thessalonians?

In other words, what does Jesus have to say about the matter and how does everything else sync with Him?

Here was my concern: after looking at history and the prophetic passages of the Old Testament prophets Daniel and Ezekiel, I needed to cross reference what the New Testament stated about the end. Specifically, what the New Testament suggested about the rapture and return of Christ.

Proper exegesis and textual criticism places importance on what Jesus says about His own return in the Olivet Discourse. With proper authority given to the words of Jesus, God incarnate, you can then interpret the messages of Paul in 1 and 2 Thessalonians and the Revelation given to John on the

Island of Patmos accurately. Since these occurred after the Olivet Discourse and fall under the authority of Christ, the passages should submit to what Christ is saying. I can't overstate the importance of properly examining the text, that the words of Paul and the vision given to John submit to the words of Christ.

Also, since the Bible is inerrant, everything that is stated from Jesus and through the messages of Paul to the Revelation given to John should sync with the prophecies of the Old Testament. To get to the heart of the matter we have to go direct to the source, to the words of Jesus, the Olivet Discourse.

Jesus Tells of His Return

In Matthew 24, as Jesus and the disciples were leaving the Temple and "going away" from it, the disciples would begin to point out the buildings of the Temple to Jesus. At this point in the passage Jesus would begin to prophesy. He would begin by speaking about the Temple and the events that would transpire within one generation of His birth.

"Jesus left the temple and was going away, when His disciples came to point out to Him the buildings of the temple. But He answered them, "You see all these, do you not? Truly, I say to you, **there will not be left here one stone upon another that will not be thrown down.**" - Matthew 24:1-2

Here we see Jesus predict the destruction of the Second Temple. It would come true through the Siege of Jerusalem in 70 A.D. One generation from His birth, the life of a king according to scripture, His words would be fulfilled and the Temple would be destroyed.

I can just envision Jesus leading the way out of the city near the Temple Mount and toward the Mount of Olives with the disciples following behind Him in stride. Many of them talking with each other and wondering if what He said would come true. As they make their ascent up to the top of the Mount of Olives they whisper amongst each other. Then reaching the summit they would sit and rest, looking out over the city. As Jesus sits they approach Him with child-like curiosity of His return.

"As He sat on the Mount of Olives, the disciples came to Him privately, saying, "Tell us, when will these things be, and what will be the sign of your coming and of the end of the age?

And Jesus answered them, "See that no one leads you astray. For many will come in my name, saying, 'I am the Christ,' and they will lead many astray. And you will hear of wars and rumors of wars. See that you are not alarmed, for this must take place, **but the end is not yet**. For nation will rise against nation, and kingdom against kingdom, and there will be famines and earthquakes in various places. All these are but the beginning of the birth pains." - Matthew 24:3-8

Here we see Jesus go on and speak toward the "Time of the Gentiles" or the gap in Daniel 9 which spans the destruction of the Second Temple to the Third Temple period. He speaks in generality about how things will continue to intensify over time after His death and resurrection until the day of His return. But what occurs during this period is just "the beginning of the birth pains" (v.8).

From here He shifts gears and we start to hear about "tribulation", a period of falling away and lawlessness increasing, the love of many growing cold and the Gospel reaching the nations.

"**Then they will deliver you up to tribulation** and put you to death, and you will be hated by all nations for my name's sake. **And then many will fall away** and betray one another and hate one another. And many false prophets will arise and lead many astray. And because lawlessness will be increased, the love of many will grow cold. But the one who endures to the end will be saved. And this gospel of the kingdom will be proclaimed throughout the whole world as a testimony to all nations, and then the end will come." - Matthew 24:9-14

Then after speaking about tribulation Christ goes on to speak specifically about an event prophesied in Daniel 9, the 70 Weeks prophecy, known as the Abomination of Desolation. This event is the formal revealing of the Antichrist, which occurs halfway through the entire Tribulation period. It marks the beginning of the Great Tribulation, which is the last 3 1/2 years of the 7 year Tribulation.

This is where we need to pay attention, as it says in the text.

"So when you see the Abomination of Desolation spoken of by the prophet Daniel, standing in the holy place (let the reader understand), then let those who are in Judea flee to the mountains. Let the one who is on the housetop not go down to take what is in his house, and let the one who is in the field not turn back to take his cloak. And alas for women who are pregnant and for those who are nursing infants in those days! Pray that your flight may not be in winter or on a Sabbath. For then there will be great tribulation, such as has not been from the beginning of the world until now, no, and never will be. And if those days had not been cut short, no human being would be saved. But for the sake of the elect those days will be cut short." - Matthew 24:15-22

Here we see Jesus directly mention the prophet Daniel and his prophecy of the 70 Weeks. Why is this? There is a specific reason.

Throughout the entire discourse Jesus has been in sync with Daniel 9. Jesus is building on the prophesy of Daniel giving specifics to what will happen in the Last Days. The Olivet Discourse occurs in Matthew 24 after Christ literally fulfills Daniel 9 in Matthew 21 during the Triumphal Entry. Jesus goes on to speak toward what will happen after He is "cut off", regarding the destruction of the Second Temple and into the final week of Daniel 9, or the Tribulation.

"Then after the sixty-two weeks the Messiah will be cut off and have nothing, and the people of the prince who is to come will destroy the city and the sanctuary. And its end will come with a flood; even to the end there will be war; desolations are determined. **And he will make a firm covenant with the many for one week....**" - Daniel 9:26-27 (NASB)

As Jesus continues to prophesy He gives specific direction about the last half of the Tribulation marked by a specific event, the Abomination of Desolation, even saying that the days are cut short for the sake of the elect. But then, after speaking about the Great Tribulation, He speaks of His return.

"But immediately after the tribulation of those days the sun will be darkened, and the moon will not give its light, and the stars will fall from the sky, and the powers of the heavens will be shaken. And then the sign of the Son of Man will appear in the sky, and then all the tribes of the earth will mourn, **and they will see the Son of Man coming on the clouds of the sky with power and great glory**. And He will send forth His angels with a great trumpet and they will gather together His elect from the four winds, from one end of the sky to the other." - Matthew 24:29-31 (NASB)

Throughout the Olivet Discourse we see that Jesus is very systematic in how He shares information regarding the Last Days. He starts with the Temple, prophesying its destruction. He then explains the Time of the Gentiles, the beginning of the Tribulation, He goes to explain the Abomination of Desolation, the subsequent Great Tribulation and finally His return.

After reading the Olivet Discourse it appears that Jesus returns after the Great Tribulation. Speaking to the Great Tribulation being cut short for the "sake of the elect" (v. 22), emphasizing the importance of taking heed the severity of the Abomination of Desolation and even giving directives to those elect who witness the event. Not only are the words of Jesus Himself significant, but also that He references Daniel 9 and speaks throughout the discourse in chronological order.

From Jesus Himself

What is so powerful about the Olivet Discourse is that Jesus Himself is prophesying, the Messiah, God incarnate. He predicts the Fall of Jerusalem which would happen 70 years after His birth. He also speaks in generality about what will occur during His absence and the "Time of the Gentiles" mentioned in Luke 21. He concludes by going back to a prophet of old, Daniel, a man who preceded Him as a forerunner and confirms through further declaration what will occur during the final week of Daniel's prophecy.

Most people look at Matthew 24 and get stuck in the middle. They miss the supernatural accuracy of Christ's prediction toward the destruction of the Second Temple or the fact that Jesus is chronologically in line with Daniel 9. We also see Jesus end with specifics related to the "Last Week" or the Tribulation. Specifically, what will happen the during the last half of the Tribulation, the Great Tribulation.

Why should our attention be peaked?

Because not only did Daniel 9 predict accurately the Triumphal Entry of Christ, Jesus goes on to confirm Daniel's prophecy and builds on it, giving clarity and specifics to the destruction of the Temple even to the Abomination of Desolation. What Christians should be aware of is that He ends with His return immediately after "the tribulation of those days".

This brings New Testament, Jesus spoken, validity to the passages of the Prophets. This means that those who look at the events prophesied by Daniel to have already been completed or see the Book of Revelation as having already occurred in history are contradicting the prophecy of Christ. These passages are foretelling the "Day of the Lord", that which occurs at the very end.

Jesus goes on to mention His coming and doesn't leave them in the dark.

"But immediately after the tribulation of those days the sun will be darkened, and the moon will not give its light, and the stars will fall from the sky, and the powers of the heavens will be shaken. And then the sign of the Son of Man will appear in the sky, and then all the tribes of the earth will mourn, **and they will see the Son of Man coming on the clouds of the sky with power and great glory**. And He will send forth His angels with a great trumpet and they will gather together His elect from the four winds, from one end of the sky to the other." - Matthew 24:29-31 (NASB)

We know that "the tribulation of those days" (v. 29) is directly referring to the last week of Daniel's 70 weeks based on the context of the passage and Jesus' reference to Daniel. But it specifically appears after the Great Tribulation, implying that the elect will not only witness the Abomination of Desolation but will endure to the end.

So, if Jesus is saying He returns after the Tribulation, are all elect left to endure till the end? Is there an early rapture of the saints before the Tribulation?

Significant Implications

As you continue to read through the Olivet Discourse you come to the end and find possibly the most popular passage related to the return of Christ. Popular because it is used by many as a way to deter the conversation of the end times or to minimize the study of the end. However, it is used out of context.

Titled, "No One Knows That Day and Hour", Matthew 24:36-51 is a passage that speaks to the days of Noah, how judgement came as a surprise to people as they were going about their daily lives. That the same will be true in the end. **However, it wasn't a surprise to Noah.** Noah was given word from God to prepare for coming judgement. His obedience to God was an act of faith, the ark a symbol of God's protection through the storm, not removal from it.

Noah was righteous and therefore in tune with God. Because of this Noah was prepared, ready and as a result was carried safely through the storm.

The passage is not talking about a surprise element for the elect, rather just the opposite. The return of Christ is a surprise element for those who are unregenerate, or even worse... Christians who are unprepared, living as in the world.

I can not stress the importance of this context enough.

The passage is about being a "faithful and wise servant" (v. 45) who is ready when the master returns. This faithful servant is given authority over all of the master's possessions. But notice what happens to the wicked servant.

"But if that wicked servant says to himself, 'My master is delayed,' and begins to beat his fellow servants and eats and drinks with drunkards, **the master of that servant will come on a day when he does not expect him and at an hour he does not know...**" - Matthew 24:48-50

In other words, the godly are in tune with God and they are prepared. The sign of wickedness is being caught off guard or surprised. Since we do not know the day or the hour of Jesus' return we should be ready. Not just in how we live and act, but also in our understanding of what Jesus said to look for.

After seeing the direct correlation of the Olivet Discourse to Daniel 9 I was confronted with these questions:

• How do the passages of Paul to the Thessalonians correlate to the Olivet Discourse and Daniel 9?
• How do these correlate to the vision of John on the

island of Patmos in Revelation 19?

• If all the passages sync, what do they suggest about the 'rapture' of the saints?

Much of what is being taught in mainstream Christianity about a Pre-Tribulation rapture wasn't appearing in the Olivet Discourse or Daniel 9. Since the Olivet Discourse is the Word spoken by God in the flesh, Jesus, before the letters of Paul to the Thessalonians and before the Revelation to John I was troubled.

The implications are severe.

Not only are we not supposed to add to the Word of God, but if there is even the slightest chance that Believers are going through the Tribulation I had to dig deeper. If there was ever a time to ask God for the Holy Spirit's discernment this would be the time. Especially if signs of the times are presenting themselves today. So I did the work and what I found was sobering.

CHAPTER 8

THE DISCOURSE - PART II

"If there is confusion on a matter then men have been involved. God does not author confusion. Return to the Bible, let the Word do the talking. What the Bible says is paramount." - Anonymous

Since God is always right it would only make sense to use the Olivet Discourse as our plumb line to test prophetic scripture in the New Testament against. The passage was from Jesus, God incarnate, and He was talking about His own return. So after seeing the direct correlation of the Olivet Discourse to Daniel 9 I was confronted with these questions:

• How do the passages of Paul to the Thessalonians correlate to the Olivet Discourse and Daniel 9?
• How do these correlate to the vision of John on the island of Patmos in Revelation 19?
• If all the passages sync up, what do they suggest about the rapture of the saints?

In other words, how does the Olivet Discourse compare to other famous, end times scripture in the New Testament? And how does it compare to mainstream teaching about the end times today?

If all the passages line up, are we in line with what they say?

As you can imagine, other passages related to the return of Christ or the Last Days submit to and fall under the teaching of Jesus. But to see this we now have to compare Matthew 24 to other key passages, namely New Testament passages given through disciples after the Ascension of Christ. To begin we will look at the words of Paul to the Church in Thessalonica.

The Confirming Message of Paul

It is located in the books of 1 and 2 Thessalonians where we see Paul address the concerns of the Last Days. What we as the reader need to understand before reading these passages is that they were spoken after Jesus and His Olivet Discourse. **Paul is building on but not adding to or changing what Jesus said.**

To compare the messages of Paul to the Thessalonians against the words of Jesus we will start in 1 Thessalonians. When we look at the message of Paul we see that what Jesus said about His return syncs perfectly with the 'rapture' account in 1 Thessalonians 4.

"For since we believe that Jesus died and rose again, even so, through Jesus, God will bring with him those who have fallen asleep. For this we declare to you by a word from the Lord, that **we who are alive, who are left until the coming of the Lord, will not precede those who have fallen asleep.** For the Lord himself will descend from heaven with a cry of command, with the voice of an archangel, **and with the sound of the trumpet of God.** And the dead in Christ will rise first. **Then we who are alive, who are left, will be** caught up together with them in the clouds to meet the Lord in the air, and so we will always be with the Lord." - 1 Thessalonians 4:14-17

Let's look again at what Jesus Himself said about His return.

"Immediately after the tribulation of those days the sun will be darkened, and the moon will not give its light, and the stars will fall from heaven, and the powers of the heavens will be shaken. Then will appear in heaven the sign of the Son of Man, and then all the tribes of the earth will mourn, and they will see the Son of Man coming on the clouds of heaven with power and great glory. And he will send out his angels with a loud trumpet call, and they will gather his elect from the four winds, from one end of heaven to the other." - Matthew 24:29-31

Those mentioned in 1 Thessalonians 4 who are asleep are Believers who have died but are in Heaven with Jesus. They are 'asleep' or dead in the body but alive in spirit with Christ. They have experienced the first death, but not the second, which is the lake of fire, the final death which they will never experience. When Jesus returns He brings those who are 'asleep' with Him.

"For since we believe that Jesus died and rose again, even so, through Jesus, God will bring with him those who have fallen asleep." - 1 Thessalonians 4:14

It is because their spirit and soul are separate from their bodies. Their bodies are raised at the return of Christ before the living saints. Then, the elect who are living are caught up in the clouds with Christ and the saints that had gone before them.

"Then we who are alive, who are left, will be caught up together with them in the clouds to meet the Lord in the air, and so we will always be with the Lord." - 1 Thessalonians 4:17

But this rapture is not prior to the Tribulation, rather, it occurs after.

Breakthrough Correlation

Probably the biggest correlation between the prophetic words of Jesus regarding His return to the testimony of the Holy Spirit is through Paul in 2 Thessalonians. It is in this passage where we again see reinforcement of the importance of the Abomination of Desolation.

"Let no one deceive you in any way. For that day will not come, unless the rebellion comes first, and the man of lawlessness is revealed, the son of destruction, who opposes and exalts himself against every so-called god or object of worship, so that he takes his seat in the temple of God, proclaiming himself to be God." - 2 Thessalonians 2:3-4

We know this passage is speaking to the Abomination of Desolation or what Jesus was referencing in the Olivet Discourse. Because of Daniel 9 we know this is halfway through the 7 year Tribulation and marks the Great

Tribulation period. We see here more reiteration that the coming of the Lord [Day of the Lord] is after the "man of lawlessness is revealed".

Remember, Jesus Himself says that His coming will be after the "tribulation of those days"...

"Immediately after the tribulation of those days the sun will be darkened, and the moon will not give its light, and the stars will fall from heaven, and the powers of the heavens will be shaken. Then will appear in heaven the sign of the Son of Man, and then all the tribes of the earth will mourn, and **they will see the Son of Man coming on the clouds of heaven with power and great glory.** And he will send out his angels with a loud trumpet call, and they will gather his elect from the four winds, from one end of heaven to the other." - Matthew 24:29-31

This section spoken by Jesus in the Olivet Discourse occurs after the Abomination of Desolation and at the end of the entire Tribulation period. What Jesus says also matches the account of His return in Revelation 19. In the Book of Revelation His return is after the Fall of Babylon (Revelation 18) or at the end of the Tribulation and before the Millennial Kingdom and final battle, Armageddon (Revelation 20).

In short, when comparing Matthew 24, 1 Thessalonians 4, 2 Thessalonians 2 and Revelation 19 we see that all accounts match. They speak to the Lord returning, and the rapture of the saints occurring at the same time, after the Abomination of Desolation and before the Millennial Kingdom.

But what about Pre-Tribulation rapture? What is that based on and why would that message be mainstream in the Church today if it were false?

Reason of Context

Pre-Tribulation rapture teaching is based on three main components:

1. The "restrainer" in 2 Thessalonians 2 being interpreted as the Holy Spirit.
2. The Holy Spirit removing restraint in 2 Thessalonians 2 as a complete evacuation from earth, causing the elect to go with Him.
3. Cross comparison of 1 Thessalonians 4:16-18 to Matthew 24:36-51, which suggests a surprise factor to Christ's return.

Since the righteous are not objects of God's wrath and the fact that scripture seems to allude to a surprise factor of Christ's return, Pre-Tribulation teaching brings all of these factors together to point to the elect being evacuated from earth before the Tribulation.

However this isn't in scripture nor is it proper exegesis.

Rather, it is taking selected text and fitting it around a posit: that the righteous will not be present during a period of judgement since they are not objects of God's wrath.

With proper textual criticism we see that the surprise element in the Olivet Discourse is not for the righteous, but for the unrighteous. Although the blood of Jesus imputes righteousness to a Believer, and we are not an object of God's wrath, this doesn't mean complete withdrawal from a time of judgement, rather protection and supernatural covering. The same proved true to the Israelites during the plagues of Egypt and at Passover, symbolic of the blood of Jesus covering God's people from the wrath sent on the unrighteous, even while they lived among them. Also through the account of Noah, who because of his righteousness heard from God about coming judgement, in faith obeyed God and as a result was prepared and carried through the storm in a boat which represents God's salvific power.

Although there is no mention of the Church past Revelation 3 this does not mean the Church is not present, it just means that the Time of the Gentiles is complete.

But isn't the Holy Spirit removed from earth during the Tribulation?

To answer this we will look in depth at 2 Thessalonians 2, which speaks to the removal of the "restrainer".

The Restrainer and Temple

Concerning the 'restrainer' mentioned in 2 Thessalonians 2:6-8, contrary to popular belief this is not referencing the Holy Spirit but rather the Archangel Michael, who in Daniel 9 & 10 is mentioned as restraining the Prince of Persia, allowing Gabriel to give Daniel the prophetic message of the Lord.

Gabriel is the messenger where as Michael is the restrainer, holding back evil so that the message of God can go forth.

"And you know what restrains him now, so that in his time he will be revealed. For the mystery of lawlessness is already at work; **only he who now restrains will do so until he is taken out of the way. Then that lawless one will be revealed**..." - 2 Thessalonians 2:6-8 (NASB)

This passage has been used in Pre-Tribulation teaching, along with Matthew 24:42-51 and 1 Thessalonians 4:16-17, to explain the "restrainer" as the Holy Spirit. That His removal is an evacuation from earth prior to the Tribulation and takes Christians with Him because they are sealed by the Holy Spirit. However, this out of context and a presumption based on inaccurate interpretation of the text. Here is why:

1. By the time the Abomination of Desolation occurs, the event 2 Thessalonians 2:6-8 is speaking about, it is halfway through the Tribulation. So at best we would be looking at a Mid-Tribulation rapture and that is based on Pre-Tribulation criteria, that the Holy Spirit is the "restrainer" and is evacuated when "taken out of the way" to reveal the "lawless one". However the revealing of the lawless one is half way through the 7 year Tribulation.

2. The Third Temple has already been built at the time 2 Thessalonians 2:6-8 is referencing, sacrifices have already been going on. Based on Ezekiel 40-42, part of the covenant

brokered between Israel and the Antichrist is the ability to rebuild the Temple on the Temple Mount. This is known as Ezekiel's Temple or the Third Temple. Regardless of how long it takes for the Temple to be rebuilt after the covenant, the Temple is rebuilt during the first half of the Tribulation, so ceremonial sacrifice is already occurring. The Abomination of Desolation is when the Antichrist **stops all sacrifices**, meaning they have already been going on. So even if the Holy Spirit is the "restrainer" mentioned in 2 Thessalonians 2, the restrainer is not removed until halfway through the Tribulation and is still present during the reconstruction of the Temple and through Tribulation ceremonial sacrifice.

Even based on Pre-Tribulation interpretation that "he who now restrains" in 2 Thessalonians 2 is the Holy Spirit, the restrainer is not removed until the Abomination of Desolation, which is halfway through the 7 year Tribulation. In the text we see clearly that the "restrainer" is present on earth throughout ceremonial sacrifice in the Temple leading up to the Abomination of Desolation.

The Holy Spirit is still very much present on earth and active during at least the first half of the 7 year Tribulation. All this means is that ceremonial sacrifices are null and void, as we already know to be true, so it doesn't mean anything. In fact, the Holy Spirit does a mighty work in Judaism during the Tribulation and many Jews turn to faith in Yeshua as the Messiah.

The Great Tribulation

We need to remember that the words of Jesus have

ultimate authority. That the words of Paul and John submit to and support the words of Jesus. Jesus speaks chronologically, referencing Daniel 9, building up to the Abomination of Desolation and into the period of the Great Tribulation. Jesus goes on to say that the period after the Abomination of Desolation is cut short for the "sake of the elect".

"And if those days had not been cut short, no human being would be saved. **But for the sake of the elect those days will be cut short.**" - Matthew 24:22

The real question is, why did Jesus say the days are cut short [Great Tribulation] for the elect if the restrainer is evacuated at the Abomination of Desolation, taking the elect with Him?

The reason is because the Holy Spirit isn't evacuated and the elect remain. The Holy Spirit remains even during the Great Tribulation. The elect are here and so is the Holy Spirit. The "restrainer" is not the Holy Spirit but rather the Archangel, Michael.

That the "restrainer" in 2 Thessalonians 2:7 is the Holy Spirit is proliferated based on incorrect word study. The gender used to describe the male which restrains is neutered, this has been viewed to mean the Holy Spirit. But also because these passages in 1 & 2 Thessalonians are taken out of context.

In Daniel 9 and 10, the passage that Jesus is referencing in the Olivet Discourse, Gabriel himself tells Daniel who is doing the restraining.

"Then he said, "Do you know why I have come to you? But now I will return to fight against the prince of Persia; and when I go out, behold, the prince of Greece will come. But I will tell you what is inscribed in the book of truth: **there is none who contends by my side against these except Michael, your prince.**" - Daniel 10:20-21

Jesus references the prophet Daniel for a reason (Matt 24:15). There is a reason why Michael is restraining the Prince of Persia in Daniel 9 and 10, which Jesus is referencing in the Olivet Discourse and Paul goes on to reference in 1 and 2 Thessalonians. **It is because Michael is the restrainer and Gabriel is the messenger.** The very same messenger that told Mary about the Christ child she was carrying, the very Christ that is referencing Daniel 9.

So in context, based on cross-section analysis and word study, Believers remain throughout the entire Tribulation period. We see that the Olivet Discourse syncs not only with what is mentioned by Paul in 1 and 2 Thessalonians but that it also matches accurately with the prophetic vision of John in Revelation 19. Jesus returns after the Tribulation and before the Millennial reign.

As mentioned above, Matthew 24:36-51 speaks to the days of Noah, how judgement came as a surprise to people as they were going about their daily lives. That the same will be true in the end. However, it wasn't a surprise to Noah.

In context Noah was given word from God to prepare for coming judgement. His obedience to God was an act of faith, the ark a symbol of God's protection through the storm, not removal from it. Noah was righteous and therefore in tune with God. Because of this Noah was prepared, ready and as a result was carried safely through the storm. The passage is not talking about a surprise element for the elect, rather just the opposite. The return of Christ is a surprise element for those who are unregenerate, or even worse... Christians who are unprepared, living as in the world.

Breaking it Down

There is no specific passage which states that the elect will be removed prior to the Tribulation. This thesis posits that the "restrainer" is the Holy Spirit. Even if this were true, the timing of 2 Thessalonians 2 is at the Abomination of Desolation, which occurs at the halfway point of the 7 year Tribulation. At best you are looking at a Mid-Tribulation rapture and that is still based on the presupposition that the "restrainer" is the Holy Spirit. But we know this is likely a misinterpretation of the text.

While there is some support for Mid-Tribulation rapture of the saints the strongest Biblical support for the timing of the rapture is Post-Tribulation, Pre-Millennial. That the rapture of the saints and the Coming of the Lord are one event. We see that when comparing the Olivet Discourse (Matthew 24, Mark 13 and Luke 21) to the words of Paul in Thessalonians and the vision of John in Revelation 19 that the rapture of the saints occurs in conjunction with Christ's return which is after the 7 year Tribulation period, before His Millennial reign.

Sadly, there is a correlation of Pre-Tribulation rapture teaching to false prophecy or teaching, telling people "everything is going to be okay, there is no need to repent" when in fact the opposite is true. Ironically, when you read all of 1 Thessalonians 4, verses 1-12 are about sanctity and holiness, living a life pleasing to God which are the garments we are to be clothed in so that we ready for His return.

There is a high probability that Pre-Tribulation rapture teaching is a deception and the reason for the "great falling away" or Great Apostasy mentioned in 2 Thessalonians 2 during the Tribulation. **Remember, this apostasy is of the elect.**

"Let no one deceive you in any way. For that day will not come, unless the rebellion comes first, and the man of lawlessness is revealed, the son of destruction, who opposes and exalts himself against every so-called god or object of worship, so that he takes his seat in the temple of God, proclaiming himself to be God." - 2 Thessalonians 2:3-4

The word "rebellion" above translates to **apostasy** or **apostasia** in the Greek. We know this passage is speaking of a great falling away of the elect prior to the Abomination of Desolation.

So leading up to the Abomination of Desolation there is a great falling away of the elect, as the "day will not come", the Second Coming of Jesus, until the lawless one is revealed. There is a high probability that Pre-Tribulation rapture teaching is the cause of this great falling away, as Believers are left unprepared and witness not only Ezekiel's Magog War but the covenant and the reconstruction of the Temple on the Temple Mount.

The Lesson of the Fig Tree - Be Prepared

The lesson is to be prepared, in spirit and truth. To be knowledgeable of the scriptures so that you are not taken by deceptive teaching. To repent and live everyday as if Christ could return. But also to be as Noah was, a righteous man that was in tune with God and as a result was prepared for when the storm came. Because of this he was carried through the storm not only by supernatural provision but because of practical obedience and preparation.

In Matthew 24, before concluding, Jesus uses the illustration of a fig tree to explain the importance of being prepared.

"From the fig tree learn its lesson: as soon as its branch becomes tender and puts out its leaves, you know that summer is near. So also, when you see all these things, you know that he is near, at the very gates." - Matthew 24:32

You may remember another fig tree, one that Jesus cursed in Matthew 21 after the Triumphal Entry.

"In the morning, as He was returning to the city, He became hungry. And seeing a fig tree by the wayside, He went to it and found nothing on it but only leaves. And He said to it, "May no fruit ever come from you again!" And the fig tree withered at once." - Matthew 21:18-19

This tree was not ready, in season or out, for Christ. Remember it was not the season for figs, but nonetheless Jesus curses the tree for not being ready with fruit. This passage of scripture is a warning to the Believer to be ready for Christ's ultimate Triumphal Entry, when He returns at the Day of the Lord (Rev 19).

In short, seasons are very important to God. He does everything on time and in season. Therefore we are called to be ready in and out of season, ever watchful for the day when He arrives. We should use discernment and walk in obedience for many, including the elect, will be deceived. This is why it is important to understand scripture, because the result of ignorance is serious. God's people die for a lack of knowledge.

What then are the signs we should look for, the 'fig tree' of our day, and are these signs occurring right now?

We will look at this in the next chapter.

CHAPTER 9

CONVERGENCE

"Storms cleanse, purge and reset. They are a phenomenon of a system that is looking to reset itself and start over. That should tell you something." - Anonymous

I was driving north on Highway 45 in Texas a few years ago and noticed a sign that said "Bridge May Ice in Cold Weather". It just so happened to be during an ice storm when I noticed the sign. I thought to myself, "That sign is there all year but I am paying attention to it today because there has been a storm." The storm had aligned with the season proving the sign to be correct.

The storm had aligned with the season proving the sign to be correct.

God gives signs through every season of His coming but what we have to pay attention to are signs that are in season. Storms happen in every season, but some signs only align with certain seasons. I paid close attention to those signs as an ice storm blanketed North Texas and bridges were iced over. It produced awareness and caution. However I pass by those signs all the time and pay little attention to them during the summer.

The sign isn't wrong during the summer, it just isn't the right season for it. It is warning you that when the conditions are right, when a storm comes in winter, the bridge will be hazardous and you need to take caution.

The same applies to prophecy.

God sends signs to His people on a regular basis about what He plans to do in the future. Because God is gracious He will send those early, before the season in which it applies. In the same way that I didn't pay attention to those signs during summer we have a tendency to only listen to God when it counts, during the storm and when we need Him in the moment. **But if we are in tune with God, in season and out, we can be prepared and ready for what He is going to do.**

I am reminded of Noah, whom was told to prepare for a storm even when it had never rained before. Even though Noah had never seen what God was speaking about, He acted in faith and that faith was used to carry him through the storm.

Regarding the seasons Jesus said to the disciples:

"He said to them, "It is not for you to know times or seasons that the Father has fixed by his own authority." - Acts 1:7

But we know by the parable of the fig tree in Matthew 24 that we are to pay attention to the signs of the times. We also know by the example of the fig tree in Matthew 21, that we should ready, in season and out, for Christ to make His ultimate Triumphal Entry.

Because of this we have to know the difference between **signs** and **events**. Up to this point we have looked at both prophecy that was fulfilled in the past and prophecy that will be fulfilled in the future. These are **events** or prophetic fulfillment whereas **signs** are phenomenon God uses to bring your attention to scripture, telling you that the event or fulfillment is soon approaching.

So what are specific examples of signs and events and how do we use the one to give insight into the other?

Let's look at some of the events that are mentioned in this book and their correlating passages:

Current Events

• The restoration and regathering of Israel into one nation. [Ezekiel 37]

Future Events

• Ezekiel's Magog War, which follows this regathering period. [Ezekiel 38 & 39]

• The covenant after Ezekiel's Magog War which formally begins the last week of Daniel 9, or the 7 year Tribulation. [Daniel 9]

• The 7 Year Tribulation. [Revelation]

• The rebuilding of the Temple on the Temple Mount. [Ezekiel 40-42]

• The Abomination of Desolation, the desecration of the Temple 3 1/2 years after the covenant between the Antichrist and Israel. [Daniel 9, Matthew 24, 2 Thessalonians 2]

• The Second Coming of Christ [Matthew 24, 1 Thessalonians 4, 2 Thessalonians 2, Revelation 19]

Since we know that the first event, the restoration of Israel into one nation, has been or is in process of being fulfilled it places our attention on what is next in scripture chronologically, which is Ezekiel's Magog War.

Signs occur before an event to front run and foretell.

As we approach the convergence of the 100th Anniversary of World War I and the 70th Anniversary of the State of Israel in 2018 we know that we are coming into a time period of Temple reconstruction based on historical trend. A time period that should be ripe for prophetic fulfillment. We also know, based on God's Word, that signs front run or foretell future events of significance.

Events are typically surrounded by signs or warnings which correlate to the scripture which will soon be fulfilled. An example of such a sign would be the birth star of Christ as seen by the Magi which would lead the wisemen to the Christ child. It also states in Joel 2 that God will use signs in the heavens as warnings of His Second Coming. So when signs are happening and it appears that all is calm, it doesn't mean that the signs are wrong, it means that the signs are pointing to a future event. **When the event takes place you are in season, at that point it will be obvious that the sign is correct.**

You may recall the Blood Moon tetrad of 2014-2015, the Year of Jubilee of 2016 or the Shemitah which was also highlighted in 2015. In this chapter I want to speak to each of these and give some concrete support and scriptural backing for what they really mean and what they suggest. Remember, the prophecy of Daniel 9 is built on the Shemitah cycle.

These signs are legitimate and they are pointing to real, future events.

The Blood Moon

Similar to how we had to look back through history to get the 'Big Picture' of what God is doing with Israel, we have to look back through history to see the true significance of signs He is using. This would apply to the the Blood Moon tetrad, the Shemitah and the Jubilee Year.

In 2014 and 2015 we became aware of the Blood Moon tetrad and the Shemitah year. Starting in 2014 we saw the beginning of a rare sequence of 4 lunar eclipses known as a tetrad.

The dates were as follows:

2014 – April 15th & October 8th
2015 – April 8th & September 28th

A lunar eclipse occurs when the sun, Earth and moon align so that the Earth's shadow falls on the moon, darkening it. As a result the moon looks red.

The blood red color of the moon is caused by refraction of sunlight by the Earth's atmosphere.

A tetrad, although rare, is not significant in and of itself. However a Blood Moon as we experienced in 2014-2015 is rare. The eclipses occurred on Jewish holy days, the first day of Passover and the first day of Sukkot (The Feast of Tabernacles). The proximity of this event with upcoming anniversaries for Israel are what is of importance. Why? Because past Blood Moon tetrads have accompanied significant events for Israel.

• The 1949-1950 tetrad occurred around the formation of Israel after World War II (1948).

• The 1967-1968 tetrad occurred around the 6 Day War (1967).

A blood moon is prophesied in end times prophecy. In particular it is mentioned in Joel 2:30-31 and Revelation 6:12. So a Blood Moon tetrad of this magnitude is a sign that a future event is coming which will fulfill some aspect of end times prophecy.

What is the specific application of the Blood Moon tetrad to our day?

Based on historical trend it has to do with the land of Israel. We see that previous tetrads have a correlation to when Israel was placed in their land, secured land (1949-1950) and expanded their territory (1967). The Blood Moon is a direct sign to Israel, because of their lunar calendar.

In the creation account God separates light on the first day but doesn't create the celestial objects until the 4th day. This is because the sun and moon were created to govern time. They are both time keepers and time tellers. The sun can tell time on a sun dial, or daily time and the moon tells monthly time.

Notice what it says in Genesis 1:14:

"And God said, "Let there be lights in the expanse of the heavens to separate the day from the night. **And let them be for signs and for seasons,** and for days and years,"

The Jewish people operate on a lunar calendar. So a moon of blood is a sign that shows they are in season for giving birth, or able to give birth. When a time keeper like the moon is red it is telling the Jewish people this: **you are in season for prophetic fulfillment**. Specifically, prophetic fulfillment related to the land, as we have seen surrounding other Blood Moon tetrads.

The Shemitah

In conjunction with the Blood Moon tetrad we learned of the Shemitah in 2015. What is the Shemitah and what are the implications?

The Shemitah is a Sabbath year, every 7th year the people of Israel are to allow the land to rest. It is a time that was proclaimed as Law in the Book of Leviticus.

"Speak to the people of Israel and say to them, when you come into the land that I give you, the land shall keep a Sabbath to the Lord. For six years you shall sow your field, and for six years you shall prune your vineyard and gather in its fruits, **but in the seventh year there shall be a Sabbath of solemn rest for the land**, a Sabbath to the Lord." - Leviticus 25:2-4

In short the Shemitah is a Sabbath rest for the land of Israel which occurs on the 7th year.

Because land has a connection to commerce and industry there has been a connection made to the 9-11 terrorist attacks in 2001, which was a Shemitah year, and to the Financial Crisis in 2008, also a Shemitah year. The Shemitah has no direct correlation to America however it is intended for the Jewish people and applicable to those living under the Jewish Law. America has the second largest number of Jews next to the State of Israel, which is likely why the Shemitah has had a significant impact here. The recent events tied to the Shemitah are likely birth pangs forerunning larger fulfillment. The Shemitah is part of a bigger picture. Remember from

Chapter 4, that God built everything on cycles or "Sets of 7". He starts the cycle at creation, it begins with 7 days and builds from there.

A refresher of the Sets of 7.

• **7th Day (Sabbath)** - God rested on the seventh day. It marks rest or Sabbath.

• **7th Year (Sabbatical Year or Shemitah)** - The 7th year the land is to rest, a sabbatical year. This set of 7 is called a Shemitah.

• **7 Sets of 7 – (Jubilee Cycle)** - After 7 sets of sabbatical years there is a Jubilee Year (50th).

• **70 Sets of 7** – A special marker given to Daniel (Chapter 9) by God. Notably, the last week (or 7 days) in this symbolic period is the 7 year Tribulation.

You may be picking up on the connection here. That the cycles ultimately build to what Daniel was prophesying, the 70 Weeks or the 70 Sets of 7. Before it gets there it goes through a cycle called a Jubilee Year. The Shemitah is just building up to something much bigger, a larger Sabbath rest for the land and the people of Israel. It is called the Jubilee Year and it has significant implications prophetically.

The Jubilee Year

In researching the Gregorian and Hebrew calendar I came across an article on Haaretz, a Jewish news magazine which provides real time news and analysis of the Middle East. They ran a story in 2015 which had a general statement, it was not intended to be earth shattering but it would shock most people... including most Christians.

It was as follows:

"Israel's official calendar is the Hebrew one. According to Jewish counting, on September 24, 2014, we entered the Year 5775, that is – the supposed 5775th year since the world was created on Saturday night, October 6, 3761 BCE." 14

Unlike the Gregorian calendar of the West, the Hebrew calendar is a lunar calendar. But also unlike the calendar of the West it counts "days since creation".

The Hebrew calendar is based on astronomy, the lunar cycle and the solstices. When God placed the sun and moon in the heavens to govern time on the 4th day of creation He also started a clock, the ability to tell time. Because of simple math, just as you can count years forward you can also count years backward.

So, if the Hebrew calendar and time keeping are correct then you should be able to track it back to when it was created, on the 4th day of creation.

I thought to myself, "Since Hebrew time keeping goes back to creation we should be able to tell if modern day sabbatical cycles (Shemitah) are accurate. We should also be able to correlate them to Jubilee Years. In other words, if

Jewish time keeping is legitimate it should all check out.".

I decided to do the work and put it to the test. I wanted to find out the following:

1. Are modern day observances of the sabbatical year (Shemitah) in line with history? In other words, if you start with the Shemitah of 5775 (Sept. 24, 2014 through Sept. 13, 2015) and track back every 7 years does it correlate accurately to the Gregorian calendar?

2. Based on modern day sabbatical year observances, do Jubilee cycles correlate? In other words, if the year 5776 is in fact a Jubilee Year and you track back to measure it does it correlate to the approximate historical era of the entrance of the Israelites into the land of Canaan?

3. Are we really in the 70th Jubilee?

4. When this is all mapped out, does it sync with historical events based on the Gregorian calendar and secular archeology/history?

So I decided to put together a spreadsheet from the most recent Shemitah (Sept. 24, 2014 through Sept. 13, 2015) and what I found was remarkable.

A video of the spreadsheet can be found on my website at mattcote.com/resources.

Based on the modern day observance of the shmita (Shemitah) I was able to not only track the Sabbatical cycles from current day to the Jewish date of creation, I was able to track Jubilee cycles to the historic period of when the Israelites would have entered the land of Canaan. It not only synced perfectly with the Gregorian account of history it synced with historical events such as the Battle of Jericho, the birth of Jesus and other historical accounts. Here is what I found:

The Shemitah or sabbatical year prior to a Jubilee cycle doesn't have the same significance as prior Shemitah years. **It is because the significance is placed on the Jubilee Year.** This is important and why seemingly nothing happened in 2015 while all the signs were pointing to something significant.

Not only are we in the 70th Jubilee, the 2 prior Jubilee Years are of monumental significance as it relates to the land of Israel.

Jubilee 68 (5678) – Gregorian Years 1917-1918 – World War I
Jubilee 69 (5727) – Gregorian Years 1966-1967 – 6 Day War
Jubilee 70 (5776) – Gregorian Years 2015-2016 – TBD

There is a specific connection.

World War I, as we covered in Chapter 3, was the beginning of the repossession of the Holy Land. It was this war where the Ottoman Empire was defeated and the land of Palestine was repossessed. But it gets even more specific. It was the Battle of Megiddo (1918) in which Allied forces would secure the land. It was the final Allied offensive of the Sinai and Palestine Campaign. This occurred in the final Gregorian year of the Jubilee.

The same would apply to the next Jubilee cycle. The next Jubilee would be year 5727 on the Hebrew calendar or 1966-1967 on the Gregorian calendar. In the final Gregorian year of the Jubilee (1967) there would be the 6 Day War. Israel would capture the Gaza Strip and Sinai Peninsula from Egypt, the West Bank and East Jerusalem from Jordan and the Golan Heights from Syria.

What does it all mean?

If history repeats itself, it means that there should be a war of significance in or around Israel in the coming years that will bring about the fulfillment of prophecy. **The overall the window of significance is 2016-2018.** The entire purpose of which is to bring about fulfillment related to the restoration of Israel and their land. The Shemitah and Jubilee are ultimately about the land and rest. Because of the correlation to the 70th Jubilee if such an event were to occur it would suggest the beginning of the completion of the restoration of Israel, leading to an increase of Aliyah or the return of Diaspora Jews from exile to Jerusalem.

If there is something for us to pull out here it is this: we should see a military movement in or around Israel which builds on 1918 and 1967. In short, a land grab or military takeover which expands the sovereign territory of Israel, building on 1967.

It also means there is likely Biblical significance to the military build up in the Middle East and the emergence of ISIL, which aims to restore the caliphate of the Ottoman Empire. Since that would undo all that God has done through both World Wars we know this is unlikely to occur.

It means ISIL is likely a catalyst for larger scale movement of unified nations against Israel in the future. An invasion such as Magog.

So when you bring all of this together what is the final conclusion, what are some scenarios and what should we be looking for?

We will look at this in the next and final chapter.

CHAPTER 10

CONCLUSION

"The God who has been sufficient until now, should be trusted to the end." - Charles Spurgeon

Believe it or not I could keep writing about this topic.

It is something that I have been studying and praying over for years. I began this project because it was too much information to fit into a blog post, the content had outgrown the container, so the logical next step was to put it into a book. In total there is more information than I could realistically fit into one book and keep it small enough for people to consume and digest properly.

As we conclude I want to provide a synopsis for each chapter regarding everything that is coming together, what it points to and what we can expect in the future. I will also include the implications for America, which I haven't had time to touch on up to this point.

Foundations

There are 4 main approaches to eschatology. They include Preterism, Historicism, Futurism and Idealism. The first two focus on historical fulfillment, the middle on future or ultimate fulfillment and the last on symbolic representation.

The "Day of the Lord" has not occurred yet, Jesus has not returned, therefore prophecy concerning the very end has not yet come to ultimate fulfillment. Prophecy is telescopic, meaning there is an initial and ultimate fulfillment. This book is focused on future or ultimate fulfillment.

Although theological pretense and systematic approaches to scripture can help us understand God's Word, clinging too closely to one viewpoint is ultimately the worship of man and becomes a stumbling block. Therefore we need the Holy Spirit to lead us into all truth, even in the things which are to come.

What we believe doesn't matter, it matters that what we believe in is true. It isn't the size of faith that matters, it is the object of our faith. If misplaced we miss by a mile. Therefore we want the Holy Spirit to lead us in our study of the end.

The Technology Gauge

Technology does not fall under Diminishing Returns but rather Accelerating Returns. Technology also has a growth curve that is linear, it does not ebb or flow and it is growing exponentially. Different than wars, rumors of wars and natural disasters which ebb and flow over time, it gives the best indicator of our trajectory. Because of this, technology gives us the best gauge or marker of our position in the timeline of history. We know based on "technological singularity" that we are approaching a key point in the history of man. This is a key difference which separates the prophetic application of yesteryear to the application of today.

For example, in the 1980's during the Cold War technology had not yet expanded to the place where we are at today, namely the Internet and digital disruption. We know through history, for instance the Gutenberg Press, that paradigm shifts in technology are linked to growth phases in the proliferation of the Gospel.

The advent of the Internet and digital disruption was such a shift and has implications of prophetic fulfillment as it relates not only to the Gospel, but to information increasing and the infrastructure for global control.

The Big Picture

When you stand back and look at history you get to see what God has already done but you also get a glimpse into the future. In doing so it gives us clarity into the 'big picture' of what God is doing and provides insight into how we can interpret and apply prophetic scripture in our day. Specifically, World War I was the beginning of the prophetic fulfillment of Ezekiel 37, or the regathering of Israel as one nation in the Last Days. The repossession of the Holy Land from the Ottoman Empire after World War I and the Battle of Meggido in 1918 was the first step. This concluded the war and set the stage for World War II.

At the end of World War II the Jews were placed back in the Holy Land, Palestine, and the State of Israel was born in 1948. They were unified as one nation which was a direct fulfillment of Ezekiel 37:22. Because of this we know that events which have transpired after this, such as the 6 Day

War, are building towards ultimate fulfillment and complete restoration of the Israelites into the Promised Land.

Nuclear Game Theory

The advent of nuclear technology and the nuclear bomb at the end of World War II sets the stage for the next world war or large scale military engagement which we know is prophesied to take place in the northern part of Israel. This war, called the Gog and Magog War, is one of two Magog wars. The first is known as "Ezekiel's Magog War" and precedes the Tribulation. There is wording that through modern day interpretation suggests nuclear fallout. The war concludes with a peace treaty which is brokered by the Antichrist between the Magog nations and Israel. This is the covenant mentioned in Daniel 9 which begins the Tribulation.

Nuclear technology presents a unique "end game" due to a military doctrine known as MAD or Mutual Assured Destruction. In short, it means that nuclear proliferation inevitably forces a peace treaty or covenant and world wide control, because the ability to destroy the world inevitably forces world peace. The second Gog and Magog War is mentioned in Revelation and is commonly referred to as "Armageddon". This is a different war led by Satan himself, which is the final war after the Millennial Reign of Christ.

The Bigger Picture

To understand the set up for prophetic application today you have to go all the way back to Creation and understand the cycles which God put in place, then you need to start with the first exile of Israel from the land, the Assyrian Captivity in 740-722 B.C. This was the beginning of the exile of the Jews from the Promised Land through the exile of the Northern Kingdom of Israel. Later Judah would be sent into exile. As a result of the Siege of Jerusalem in 597 B.C. Jews would be sent into the Babylonian Captivity. As prophesied by the prophet Jeremiah, the Jews would be held captive in Babylon for 70 years. The prophet Daniel was in the first wave of deportation and the prophet Ezekiel was in the second wave.

In captivity Daniel would prophesy a very specific piece of prophecy known as the 70 Weeks. Also in exile Ezekiel would begin to prophesy about the regathering of Israel during the Last Days and toward a future Temple known today as Ezekiel's Temple. Daniel's prophecy, the 70 Weeks, predicted with supernatural accuracy the Triumphal Entry of Christ, 483 years after the proclamation of Artaxerxes I in 445 B.C. to rebuild Jerusalem. It also predicted the death of Christ and the destruction of the Second Temple. This leads us into the Time of the Gentiles, mentioned in Luke 21. Towards the end of the Time of the Gentiles occurs what I call the Ezekiel 37-39 Window.

The Ezekiel 37-39 Window

Just as the prophecy of Daniel would build on the prophecy of Jeremiah, the prophecy of Ezekiel would build on the prophecy of Daniel. There is a gap in the prophecy of Daniel 9 between the destruction of the Second Temple and the covenant between Israel and the Antichrist, which makes way for the rebuilding of the Third Temple (Ezekiel 40-42). This is known at the Time of the Gentiles or the Age of Grace, mentioned in Luke 21. We know based on Ezekiel 37 that there is a restoration of Israel to their land. This occurs after the destruction of the Second Temple prophesied in Daniel 9 and towards the end of the gap, before the last week or the 7 year Tribulation.

As we looked at in the chapter titled "The Big Picture", the restoration of Israel after World War I and World War II was the fulfillment of this prophecy, it completed what had not been since well before the Assyrian Captivity, which is a unified Israel as one nation (Ezekiel 37:22). The Ten Lost Tribes are now returning to Israel. Because of this we know that Ezekiel's Gog and Magog War is next. Due to our place in history it would be wise to know exactly what Ezekiel's Magog is, what nations are involved and how it ends. This war precedes the Tribulation.

The Final Wars

Ezekiel's Gog and Magog War is between a very specific group of nations in the Middle East. The list of nations include:

Gog (or Rosh) = Russia
Magog = Turkey
Meshech & Tubal = Turkey & Georgia
Gomer & Beth-togarmah = Turkey
Persia = Iran
Put = Libya
Cush = Ethiopia or Sudan

Ezekiel's Gog and Magog War is led by Gog (Rosh), a leader from the North which we can historically and contextually identify as modern day Southern Russia or the Black Sea region. However "Magog" literally translates to Asia Minor or modern day Turkey, which is the staging ground for this decent into Israel from the North. Israel wins handily and text suggests either supernatural intervention from God or the use of WMD's, specifically long lasting fallout from something like a nuclear weapon, which forces a peace treaty or covenant. At the end of this war the Antichrist makes a covenant or peace treaty with the Magog nations and Israel. This is the beginning of the 7 year Tribulation.

The Gog and Magog War in Revelation is after the Millennial Reign of Christ. Satan is loosed from captivity and leads a charge against Jesus and the elect. The use of "Magog" in this context translates to a "uniting of nations" or United Nations. This would explain why the United Nations was formed after World War II and why they are the governing body responsible for the State of Israel. In Revelation, Chapter 2, Pergamum is the literal "seat of Satan" which was located in literal Magog or Asia Minor.

Because of these correlations it is highly likely that the seat of Satan, or the governing body where the Antichrist will rule from and broker the covenant mentioned in Daniel 9, is the United Nations. The governing body which created Israel ultimately has authority of the state it created. In short, Magog is a uniting of nations against Israel, which has authority over Israel and turns against Israel and ultimately against Jesus in the end.

As we approach the 70 year anniversary of the State of Israel, their restoration and regathering after World War II, it means that we are entering into a period of Temple reconstruction as defined by Biblical, historical trend.

• We see this with David, whom was not allowed to build the First Temple because of the blood on his hands from war. As a result, the task would be given to the next generation, Solomon's generation. David would live exactly 70 years, which was a generation as defined by the the life of a king.

• We also see this in the Babylonian Exile. Where as Jeremiah prophesied, the Israelites would remain in exile for 70 years before returning to the land. This happened exactly as Jeremiah prophesied, the Jews would return exactly 70 years later as marked by the period of time which spanned the destruction of the First Temple and the beginning of construction on the Second Temple.

• Again we see this through the birth of Christ, where within 70 years of His brith the prophesied destruction of the Second Temple would occur in 70 A.D.

Since the State of Israel was reborn in 1948, it means that we are approaching the end of a generation marked by the life of a king, which God uses to gap one prophetic fulfillment to another. Since the 100 year anniversary of World War I coincides in 2018, in the coming years we are ripe for Biblical fulfillment. Mostly likely, that we will see Ezekiel's Magog War and enter into the Tribulation.

The Discourse I & II

Now that we know what the prophets of the Old Testament say about the Last Days we have to look at the New Testament and compare. Correct exegesis would apply proper authority to the words of Christ, as well as historical timing of other passages referencing the coming of the Lord. Because of this we have to look at Matthew 24, or the Olivet Discourse, spoken by God incarnate, Jesus Himself, as the plumb line to the ordering of end times events.

Just as Daniel would build on Jeremiah and Ezekiel would build on Daniel, Jesus would pick up and reference the prophecy of Daniel. Jesus would systematically go through the events that would unfold from the Destruction of the Second Temple, to the Time of the Gentiles, the Tribulation and to the Abomination of Desolation. He goes on to speak of His return after the "tribulation of those days" but specifically that the Great Tribulation, the 3 1/2 years after the Abomination of Desolation which are cut short for the "sake of the elect".

When we look at 2 Thessalonians 2 we see that the "restrainer" is more likely referring to Michael the Archangel who restrains the Prince of Persia so that Gabriel can deliver messages for the Lord. This syncs with Daniel 9 and 10. When speaking to the one who restrains the man of lawlessness the gender type of the word "he" is neutered male because it is referencing an angel, not the Holy Spirit. Even if the Holy Spirit were the "restrainer" in 2 Thessalonians 2 and when removed was evacuated from earth along with the elect, He is not removed until the

Abomination of Desolation which is halfway through the 7 year Tribulation period.

When you properly cross reference the Olivet Discourse to 1 Thessalonians 4, 2 Thessalonians 2 and Revelation 19 they all sync and say the same thing: that the return of Christ is after the Tribulation and before the Millennial reign of Christ. Those who are asleep, dead in the body but alive with Christ, come with Jesus at His return and their bodies are raised to meet them in the air. The elect who remain, who have not taken the Mark of the Beast, are raised afterward to meet Jesus and the saints who have gone before them in the air. We who are alive will not precede those who have 'fallen asleep' as it says in 1 Thessalonians 4.

When you look at Matthew 24:36-51 the surprise element is not for the righteous, for Noah was forewarned and prepared. God carried him through the storm. The surprise element is for the unrighteous or elect that are unrepentant and not in tune with God. In short, there is really no Biblical case for Pre-Tribulation rapture. The thesis is based on passages which are taken out of context in order to support the claim that the Church is not an object of God's wrath and therefore could not go through the Tribulation. However there is no contextual evidence based on appropriate exegesis which supports this.

Even if the Holy Spirit were the "restrainer" He is not removed until the Abomination of Desolation which is halfway through the 7 year Tribulation. But through appropriate textual criticism we see that the words of Jesus, God incarnate, preceded the message of Paul to the

Thessalonians and preceded the vision given to John on the Island of Patmos.

When put together they all say the same thing: that the elect will endure until the end of the Tribulation, then Christ will return to set up His Kingdom on earth.

Convergence

The fig tree that Jesus curses in Matthew 21 at His Triumphal Entry is symbolic of people who are not prepared, in season or out, with fruit at His ultimate Triumphal Entry or Second Coming. We are to be prepared in season and out for Christ to return and we should not be caught off guard. In Matthew 24 Jesus mentions the fig tree again, to take notice of it for hints of the season. **We don't know the season, but God will gives us signs.** Signs and events are separate things. God will give signs which point to the event. We often only take heed of the sign during the storm or after the event it was intended for.

When looking at the Shemitah, the Blood Moon tetrad and the 70th Jubilee we see a correlation between all three which is land. The Shemitah signifies rest for the land, the Blood Moon tetrad has correlation to wars in which Israel was given their land or advanced their territory toward original borders. The 70th Jubilee is also about the land, specifically returning to the land. It has not been celebrated since all tribes were living in the land prior to the Assyrian Captivity. **In the Year of Jubilee the Jews are to return to their land.**

All three have the correlation of land which suggests that all three signs occurring from 2014-2016 are a sign that a significant change will be coming to the land of Israel regarding their land or sovereign territory.

Based on tracking the Jubilee Years on the Hebrew Calendar we see that there is a correlation between the Jubilee Year and land being taken, a correlation to Ezekiel 37. Specifically that the last Gregorian year tied to the Jubilee an event or military move occurs in Israel where Israel retains more of the original Promised Land. Since we are in the 70th Jubilee there is a likelihood that what is coming brings forth the final stages of Aliyah, the migration of Jews back to Israel.

Scenario and Personal Evaluation

Based on all of these factors, if history were to repeat itself, we will see major events in Israel over the coming years. The overall window of importance for a pivot in the Middle East is 2016-2018. There is a high likelihood, after this period, that we will see Israel take back land and rebuild the Temple on the Temple Mount.

We know that 2015 was likely a year of foreshadowing, with the IDF storming the Temple Mount to calm a conflict in the Al Asqa mosque on the Shemitah in Israel.

This is also why the Palestinian flag was raised at the UN that same month. Specifically there should be an event in Israel soon which builds on 1918 and 1967 and expands the sovereign territory of Israel. This event may be significant and a land claim which causes international uproar.

It all suggests that we are entering into a transitionary period.

Just as when the winter changes to spring and there are severe storms, this transitionary period should be a large scale storm that will affect the world. It should begin at the epicenter.

Times of transition are also seasons of harvest.

Specifically this transition is the completion of the regathering of the Ten Lost Tribes of Israel or the final stages of Ezekiel's restoration prophecy. It means that all which is occurring in the Middle East is likely the beginning of Ezekiel's Magog War, or at least the beginnings of the formation of the consortium which is a large scale invasion and war against Israel. It suggests this war occurring before or around 2018 leading us into the Tribulation. Of course, we will know if this is true if the war commences and a covenant is signed with Israel which allows them to rebuild the Temple on the Temple Mount.

It means that ISIL is likely just a catalyst for greater military movement, a cause to bring the world together. Arab Spring and everything that has taken place in the Middle East after World War II has been moving us to this point in history.

Regarding America

As a result of World War II the Unites States of America rose to world power. It was a transition of power from Great Britain [World War I] to America [World War II]. The United

Kingdom would pass the torch to the United States. We have been a world power ever since. It should be noted that the United Nations is also headquartered here.

Since America is the seat of world power, either America is the "Mystery Babylon" in Revelation and the Antichrist rises from here to lead the United Nations or America is neutralized as a world power and the seat of power shifts once again, back to the geographic location of the old Roman Empire. America is still a colonized extension of Great Britain (the Roman province of Britannia) with connection to the Old Roman Empire. Time will tell, but America itself is not mentioned in scripture by name, unless we are the "Mystery Babylon" mentioned in Revelation. There is a good chance that is true.

The Star of David

What most don't realize is that the Star of David or "Seal of Solomon" is really an occult symbol, analogous with the pentagram. Adopted by Zionists from Kabbalah, this occult symbol was rooted in Arabic medieval literature and based on the legend of Solomon's signet ring. The symbol is not Jewish at all, it is an abomination. It was given to Israel as their official mark by the United Nations in 1948. However it is rooted in the occult and points to the Temple. It points to Ezekiel's Temple, a common theme in the occult, for it is where the Abomination of Desolation will occur.

Most importantly the transferred mark or symbol is a veiled reference to the authority the United Nations has over the State of Israel. That the entity which created the State of

Israel has ultimate authority to broker the covenant mentioned in Daniel 9, that which begins the Tribulation and paves the way for Ezekiel's Temple.

In Closing

Regarding the peace treaty or covenant between the Magog nations and Israel, it is the UN which has governing authority over the State of Israel. The entity which created the State of Israel ultimately has power over Israel, the power to change territory lines or to broker the covenant required to begin the Tribulation.

The Bible gives us hint that this is the case. Pergamum as mentioned in Revelation 2 was noted to be, at that time, the literal "seat of Satan" in John's exhortation to the Church in Pergamum. Pergamum was located in Asia Minor or literal Magog. Since in context "Magog" in Revelation is a united nations against Jesus, we have contextual support for the United Nations being the seat of leadership where the Antichrist will lead from and broker such a covenant. Similar to the need for the Nuclear Security Summit, nuclear proliferation and security will force the hand of world peace.

All signs indicate that 2018 will be a pivotal year for the Middle East, setting in motion events that could lead to the beginning of the Tribulation and the reconstruction of the Temple. This also suggests that the fulfillment of Ezekiel 37 may occur around this same timeframe, with Ezekiel's Magog War (chapters 38-39) potentially unfolding in the near future. While this is a significant claim, it reflects the direction in which events seem to be heading.

The purpose is awareness rather than prediction.

As it relates to the Tribulation, based on proper Biblical exegesis, the Bible states that the elect go through the entire 7 year Tribulation. If the "restrainer" mentioned in 2 Thessalonians 2 is the Holy Spirit then at best we are looking at a Mid-Tribulation rapture of the saints. However this doesn't sync with scripture as there is no account of Christ coming back twice, only once. **In other words, there aren't two "Second Comings", just the First Advent and Second Advent of Christ.**

This means that the great falling away mentioned in 2 Thessalonians is likely caused buy false teachings that are being proliferated today. Specifically Pre-Tribulation rapture and other teachings which give people a feeling of apathy toward holiness and create an unrepentant worldly mindset. A lulling to sleep which will catch them off guard, pursuing the things of the world, when they should be on watch. Ironically, the entire first part 1 Thessalonians 4 is about being prepared in holiness, purity and the garments we are to be clothed in for the wedding feast. It is the opposite of a passive approach to the Almighty and His return, but rather a reverent obedience in loving submission.

Personal Response

I will close with this final message directed to my fellow Believers.

Regardless of what happens and how it is timed, we are to be ready today. Signs are emerging that we are on the precipice of global change with prophetic implications. That the end is in fact near.

This is a wake up call. To awaken you from your slumber and to prepare your heart for what is to come.

The call is to "come out from her" those who live in 'Babylon', to leave the world and all the lust that is in her. To flee from sexual immorality, from the lifestyle that is one foot in the world and one foot in the presence of God. For the fence sitters, hypocrites, and backsliders to be awakened by truth. For awakening and revival to commence among us, in the authority of Jesus' name.

For Christians to rise up in courage and to take hand to plow. To charge into the dark areas of our cities with the light of God and to cast the enemy out, bringing with them the hope and truth of the Gospel. To realize the victory which is ours in Christ and to leave a mark and legacy not just for a lifetime but for an eternity in the name of Jesus Christ.

For the Church to rise up and realize that this is our finest hour, our hour of greatness is at hand. You have everything you need to conquer the days ahead, because we are more than conquers and Christ is with us.

It is all about Jesus.

I am thankful for all He has done and all He will continue to do.

"...For the testimony of Jesus is the spirit of prophecy." - Revelation 19:10

THE GOSPEL

After reading this book you may be wondering what you should do to prepare. The future and its timing are ultimately in the hands of God.

Life is not guaranteed, it is a gift.

Because of this we are to prepare our hearts today, the Bible says that today is the day of salvation. Since every day is a gift we should seize the opportunity, not to live it for ourselves but to live it for God.

There is no name under Heaven by which man can be saved, it is only Jesus that can save you. Jesus was more than a prophet and a good man, He is God. He came to earth and lived a sinless life, His death paid the penalty for our sins. Because He was raised from the dead we can now live forever with Him.

Today you can experience the freedom of having all your sins forgiven, to feel the love and power of God, to become a new person. If you acknowledge that you have sinned and need forgiveness then you must confess it, pray to God and ask in Jesus' name for forgiveness. Place your faith and trust in Jesus. Turn from your sins and run to Jesus, He will save you.

If this is you, then pray this to God.

Next page...

"God, I am a sinner. I have sinned against you and others. Please forgive me of my sins. Jesus I believe that you are the Son of God. You are Lord and my Savior, I open my heart to you and ask that you would dwell within me. Change me from the inside out. Thank you for loving me. I want to know you more. In Jesus' name, Amen."

ABOUT THE AUTHOR

Matt Cote is a Christian author, speaker, and strategist dedicated to sharing biblical truth with modern-day relevance.

A graduate of Appalachian State University with a Bachelor of Science in Business Administration in Economics, Matt combines his understanding of economics and eschatology with a heart for biblical teaching to address today's most pressing cultural and spiritual issues.

As a writer, Matt specializes in exploring the intersection of faith and current events, with a particular focus on Israel, geopolitics, business, and macroeconomics.

Matt is the Founder & CEO of Fire Source Media, a digital marketing agency based in Waco, TX with offices in Dallas and Austin. He is also the Founder of Concept Church, a digital ministry focusing on online evangelism. For more info visit conceptchurch.com.

He and his wife Hannah live in central Texas with their two sons.

To connect with Matt, you can send him a message at mattcote.com.

NOTES

1. https://www.goodreads.com/work/quotes/18940727-preparing-for-jesus-return-daily-live-the-blessed-hope
2. https://en.wikipedia.org/wiki/Christian_eschatology
3. https://en.wikipedia.org/wiki/Diminishing_returns
4. https://commons.wikimedia.org/wiki/File:PPTMASSuseInventionsLogPRINT.jpg
5. http://www.theverge.com/2016/2/17/11032004/x-prize-ai-contest-ibm-watson-ted-2020
6. https://en.wikipedia.org/wiki/Ottoman_Caliphate
7. https://en.wikipedia.org/wiki/Mutual_assured_destruction
8. https://en.wikipedia.org/wiki/Mutual_assured_destruction
9. http://www.nytimes.com/interactive/2015/10/16/world/middleeast/untangling-the-overlapping-conflicts-in-the-syrian-war.html?_r=0
10. https://en.wikipedia.org/wiki/Babylonian_captivity
11. https://en.wikipedia.org/wiki/Nehemiah
12. http://www.ynetnews.com/articles/0,7340,L-4609941,00.html
13. http://www.chabad.org/library/article_cdo/aid/513212/jewish/When-is-the-next-Jubilee-year.htm
14. http://www.haaretz.com/jewish/high-holy-days-2014/.premium-1.617185

www.ingramcontent.com/pod-product-compliance
Lightning Source LLC
LaVergne TN
LVHW051410080426
835508LV00022B/3023